THE CHICK MAGNET

COOKING FOR HER

BOB KAPLAN

outskirts
press

The Chick Magnet
Cooking for Her
All Rights Reserved.
Copyright © 2019 Bob Kaplan
v2.0

The opinions expressed in this manuscript are solely the opinions of the author and do not represent the opinions or thoughts of the publisher. The author has represented and warranted full ownership and/or legal right to publish all the materials in this book.

This book may not be reproduced, transmitted, or stored in whole or in part by any means, including graphic, electronic, or mechanical without the express written consent of the publisher except in the case of brief quotations embodied in critical articles and reviews.

Outskirts Press, Inc.
http://www.outskirtspress.com

ISBN: 978-1-4787-7791-5

Cover Photo © 2019 www.gettyimages.com. All rights reserved - used with permission.
Interior Illustrations © 2019 Kersti Frigell. All rights reserved - used with permission.

Outskirts Press and the "OP" logo are trademarks belonging to Outskirts Press, Inc.

PRINTED IN THE UNITED STATES OF AMERICA

Dedication

To Susan

My Wonderful and Beautiful Wife

(Proof of Concept!)

TABLE OF CONTENTS

Introduction...I

Chapter I: Cooking 101 1

    Minimum Equipment 1

    Big Items...2

    Smaller Items..2

    Pots & Pans..3

    Tools & Gadgets 4

    Supplies...5

    Staples...5

    Consumables...6

    Cooking 6

    Food Handling...7

    Heat..8

    Wet Heat..8

    Dry Heat...9

Chapter II: Courting (First Impressions) 11

    A Little Homework! 11

    Table Settings 12

    Greetings...14

    Cooking and Presentation 14

    Preparation...16

    Clean As You Go! 17

Chapter III: Foreplay..18
    Wine..18
    Cocktails: (A very Feudian term) 22
    Here are Some of the Most Popular Cocktails
        For the Ladies:...24

Chapter IV: T & A (Tapas & Appetizers) 30
    Cold Appetizers..31
    Some Preparation 32
    Hot Appetizers 33

Chapter V: S & M (Soups, Salads, Sandwiches, and More) 37
    Soups 37
    Hot Soups...38
    Cold Soups..42
    Salads 46
    Sandwiches...51

Chapter VI: Intercourse (The Pause That Refreshes) 57

Chapter VII: The Main Event - Meat.........................59
    Beef...60
    Veal...64
    Lamb...70

Chapter VIII: The Main Event - Chicken....................77
    Roasting..78
    Chicken - Grilling (Barbequing).........................81
    The French Kiss: A Delight on your Tongue.........83
    The Blue Bird of Happiness! 86

Chapter IX: Seafood - Fish 90
    Salmon..91
    Seafood - Tuna 95

Chapter X: A Little on the Side 99

    Potatoes...99

    Green Veggies...103

    Pasta...110

Chapter XI: A Happy Ending - Dessert............................114

Chapter XII: B & B(Bed & Breakfast).............................121

    Cooked Breakfast 123

    Something a Little Fancier...129

    Pancakes from Scratch...134

    Breakfast Meats 135

    Even Fancier..136

    Additional Fancy Suggestions: 138

Chapter XIII: Finale..140

Appendix

    Aphrodisiacs: The Food That Excites............................144

INTRODUCTION

Cooking is an act of love.
– Jacques Pepin

What the world doesn't need now is another cookbook! My library at home contains a few hundred of them, there are thousands more that I do not own, and every day more show up in bookstores. So why am I contributing to this glut?

I had a particular audience in mind when I decided to write this cookbook—a large audience that I feel has been neglected. Although there are plenty of celebrity chefs out there who are men, their cookbooks are not aimed at your everyday Great Guy who wants to learn how to whip up dinner for a certain someone. I wrote this cookbook because I am fortunate enough to have enjoyed quite a bit of positive feedback whenever I've served a meal to a member of the fairer sex. With *The Chick Magnet*, I want to share some tricks of the trade with all those fellows out there who have never had the distinct (and rewarding) pleasure of saying, "Please come to the table, dinner is being served."

[PS] I also wrote this book for ladies, because many women have told me that they are interested in meeting a someone who knows his way around the kitchen.

Some of you may be asking yourselves, "Why cook at home? If I want to impress a lady, I'll take her out to a fancy restaurant." Well, here are a few reasons:

- You can create the exact atmosphere you want, i.e. music, candles, lights, decor, etc., at your place.

- The table is yours for as long as you like. In a restaurant they need to "turn" the table after a certain amount of time.

- It's not crowded at home, and you can hear each other speaking without having to shout.

- You don't have to be ruled by the waiter's timetable.

- It's a shorter distance to the bedroom from the dining room table than from a restaurant table.

PQ: ["Writing a cookbook is like writing a sex manual."]

"Writing a cookbook is like writing a sex manual," said Amanda Hesser, who, at the time, was the food editor of the *NY Times Magazine*, at a writers' conference a few years ago in Sun Valley, Idaho. When I told my wife that I wanted to write my cookbook as if I were writing a sex manual - not that I know what one is like - she quickly corrected me: "Write it like you'd write a seduction manual." She also said that all of you guys incorrectly think that sex and seduction are the same thing. How she knows what a seduction manual is like, I'm not sure, but I didn't press the issue.

The first meal I ever made for a female was actually for two—my sisters. Initially I had to cook to survive! My mother (may she rest in peace) was a terrible cook. She was from England. Need I say more? In fact, when she did cook, we could tell when dinner was ready, as the smoke alarm would go off. She was such a bad cook that in our house we prayed after the meal, rather than saying grace before it.

However, my mother enjoyed entertaining, and usually had a big pot of something (many times we couldn't tell what it was) on the stove on Sundays. I remember one particular Sunday when a group of my parents' friends dropped by the house in the afternoon and were still there as evening approached. Ever the gracious hostess, my mother invited them to stay for supper. Then she pulled my sisters and me aside and said that because there wasn't enough food for all of them and all of us, when the main course was served, we were to say we weren't hungry. We didn't mind passing on the mystery stew, but when she brought out the dessert and announced that anyone who had skipped the entree wouldn't get any dessert, we were dumbfounded (and not just a little hungry!).

Soon after that, I decided to take charge of the situation and start cooking. My sisters and I brokered a 50/50 deal: I made the mess and they cleaned up.

At first I stuck to the basics, but it didn't take long until I started cooking complicated dishes. I learned from my mistakes and had a lot of fun experimenting. Over the years, I relied less and less on recipes and more on instinct. When I started cooking for females other than my sisters, the stakes got a little higher. I wanted to impress my guest without spending too much money or too much time shopping, prepping, cooking . . . or cleaning up after the meal, so I focused on meals that met those criteria and delivered. This cookbook contains the most reliable (simple, but with a "wow" factor) dishes I created or adopted along the way.

The guiding principle for including recipes in *The Chick Magnet* is **KISS:**

> (Oh, how appropriate!)
> *Keep It Simple, Stupid!*

While being simple to prepare, the dishes had to present enough flair (sex appeal) to intrigue and/or impress, use ingredients that were readily available and not too expensive, and lend themselves to easy clean-up. Most of them can be prepared ahead of time so you can spend the beginning of the evening talking with or otherwise engaging your guest rather than fussing in the kitchen.

All the recipes are written to serve either two or four people. I remember eating a truly outstanding dessert while on vacation in Bermuda, and thinking that I wanted to include the recipe in my cookbook. My friends and hosts, Jeff and his comely wife, Fiona, knew the chef of the restaurant, who agreed to share his recipe for "sticky toffee pudding." Once I got home, I realized the recipe was written to make 100 servings, which is the only reason you won't find it in these pages.

When shopping for the ingredients for your special meal, or any meal, don't skimp! You can keep expenses down by avoiding exotic or out-of-season items, but stack the deck in your favor by choosing the best ingredients you can afford. Buy fresh, buy local, buy quality. Talking about "sourcing" your ingredients in this way, by the way, is guaranteed to impress any female dinner guest.

My suggested menus are crafted to inspire an evening of romance and/or friendship. That brings to mind an expression my freshman English professor taught me: "It's not how long you make it, it's how you make it long." He was referring to sentence development, but just in case you have jumped to some other conclusion, I'll point out that I am referring to the importance of drawing out the evening. Relax and enjoy the journey. Have another glass of wine between courses, or discuss the music that's playing. Being creative in this area is easier if you feel confident that the food you are about to serve is under control.

I would be remiss if I did not mention all the wonderful people who have helped me with this book. It takes a village to write a cookbook! There are those who inspired, encouraged, suggested recipes, tested recipes, suggested content, added comic relief, illustrated, edited, proofread, and of course those who nagged or embarrassed me to get it done. Many friends, both male and female, willingly shared their "proven" and favorite bachelor/bachelorette recipes with me. I try to give credit where credit is due, but please forgive me if I've miss some well-deserved acknowledgments.

And last but not least, I want to thank everyone who promised to buy it. Please follow through!

I'd like to mention a few specific people who were very important to the completion of this opus.

- Susan, my wife: chief inspiration, nag, critic, taster, supporter and critical editor,
- Meredith Alexander & Matt Kaplan: my raison d'être,
- Bridget Horstmann, my Author Representative, Outskirt Press,
- Cheri Miller, Production Manager, Outskirt Press
- Kersti Frigell, Illustrator Supreme!
- Joan Rogers, Extraordinary and helpful Editor.

Some Important thoughts:

- *BE BOLD*
- *BE CREATIVE*
- *EXPERIMENT—DON'T BE AFRAID TO TRY DIFFERENT THINGS*
- *GO NUTS*
- *HAVE FUN*
- *WEAR NICE UNDERWEAR*

CHAPTER I

COOKING 101

Cooking Is a Craft. Learn Your Medium, and Then Expand into an Art Form.

Most cookbooks give you a whole long list of recipes—what I hope to do is to certainly give you lots of recipes, but in this initial chapter I want to introduce the reader to a little knowledge about the basics of cooking. This includes some necessary equipment, food handling, preparing, cooking, and presentation. Food must appeal to many of our senses: sight, smell, taste, and touch.

I am not trying to make you into a "chef"—leave that for the culinary schools. I want to help you have fun and entertain…and impress! Cooking is not a destination, it is a journey, and in this case, a journey with a destination.

If you are already familiar with cooking and feel comfortable in the kitchen as well as entertaining, then you may want to skip this chapter, as it is really an introductory discussion on what you need and how to prepare for that special evening.

MINIMUM EQUIPMENT

As a lady friend of mine likes to say, "You can judge a guy by his equipment!"

1

A few years ago, my wife and I went to Italy to attend a cooking school. It was a ten-day course in which we cooked each morning and toured the Italian countryside in the afternoons. On one of our stops in Florence we came across a "kitchen equipment" store. Of course, I had go in and see what cooking gadgets they had. If you hadn't guessed already, I am a gadget freak! Well, as we wondered through the store examining everything, my Susan picked up something strange-looking to her and asked if we had one of these. I had to confess that we actually had two. This particular utensil was a food mill. After considerable time and our examination of just about everything in the store, she finally stumped me. She found a "pasta tester." It looked like a combination of an hors d'oeuvre fork and a petit spoon. Well, in all her sweetness, she bought it for me. Now my life—and kitchen equipment - is complete!

BIG ITEMS

I would suggest you have a stove, oven, and refrigerator! Next on my list of desirables would be a microwave oven.

A barbecue grill is always an impressive way to cook and some of the included recipes will call for barbecue grilling.

A blender is a very handy appliance for many tasks, especially mixing drinks.

Don't forget a table and chairs!

SMALLER ITEMS

KNIVES: Minimum suggested.

First of all, you need something for cutting! My suggestion is to get some reasonably good knives. It is worth the investment, as you will be using them constantly and good knives will save you a lot of effort.

Also, they will last a long time.

- 8-inch or 10-inch chef s knife,
- Serrated bread knife
- Paring knife
- Sharpening steel
- Kitchen scissors
- Vegetable peeler
- Cutting board(s)

You should not put your knives in the drawer, as the blades will get knocked and dulled. It is worthwhile buying a knife block or use a magnetic strip to hold them. Also after each use and cleaning (DO NOT PUT THEM IN THE DISHWASHER), give them a few strokes with the steel to help keep the edge.

POTS & PANS

There are numerous varieties of pots and pans, but the basic non-stick type is the most convenient (the heavier, the better).

- Two sauce pans with lids (one small and one medium)

Remember you are cooking for only two or at the most four people. If you are planning on cooking for her whole family, roller derby team, roster of friends, or Facebook directory, then you will need a third large saucepan or stockpot with lid. But I don't recommend this in the beginning. Polish up your cooking skills first.

- Skillet/frying pan (medium-sized, nonstick)
- Roasting pot with rack (small to medium)
- Baking sheet (s)
- Set of mixing bowls
- Sieve (small mesh strainer)

I have to admit, I have many more of these, but certainly do not use all of them. They just seemed to accumulate over the years. I have been tempted to clear out a lot, but for some reason never seem to get around to it—YET.

TOOLS & GADGETS

You may not have all of them; improvise and do the best you can.

I love gadgets. For example, I collect different types of corkscrews and wine decanters. But let me try to keep this list to just what is really needed. I could get carried away, but there seem to be enough checks and balances with my reviewers to keep me in line.

- Bottle openers: a combination corkscrew and church key is most convenient
- Grater: for cheeses, vegetables, and any other needs you may have
- Vegetable peeler
- Can opener
- Spatula(s)
- Measuring cups & spoons
- Whisk

- Mixing/stirring spoon
- Ladle
- Salt shaker

Optional but convenient:

- Pot holder/oven mitts
- Trivet
- Timer
- Instant-read thermometer
- Pepper grinder

SUPPLIES

There are a number of basic ingredients that are fairly common to many recipes. It is best to keep a small supply of these on hand. Do not buy too large a quantity, as some of them will not age very well. It is better to buy fresh supplies every so often. For example, good olive oil should be used within a year of processing, as it deteriorates in quality after about a year. Check the dates on ingredients when you buy them.

STAPLES

Rolls of:

- Plastic wrap, Paper towels, Aluminum foil
- Plastic bags (food savers and garbage bags)
- Salt (kosher style) & peppercorns (if you have a way to crush or grind them; otherwise buy small amounts of ground pepper. It loses its potency after a short period of time).
- Kitchen towels

- Extra virgin olive oil (I'm not sure I know what an "extra virgin" is but in any case the term is used to describe a certain quality of olive oil that has less than .5% acidity. It is the top of the line.)

- Butter—don't use margarine. First of all it is not very healthy and secondly it does not taste nearly as good.

- Red wine vinegar: If you want to splurge, get a red wine and a balsamic vinegar. There are other types as well, but these two will cover most situations.

- Dijon mustard

- Fresh garlic. Keep it in the freezer! It stays fresher longer and actually concentrates the flavor. However, use sparingly unless your lady friend also likes it, as it is known as "nature's form of birth control."

- Coffee and tea

- Sugar

- Flour

- Salt and pepper

COOKING

Cooking is really not a very complicated endeavor, although there is a lot of mystique and romance associated with it. In reality, it is just preparing the food properly (mise-en-place), applying heat to food products to enhance the taste and to soften the texture, as well as perhaps adding some seasoning, and then presentation. In some cases, you don't even apply heat—you just serve raw and/or with a sauce or dressing. And of course, an important part of cooking for someone is the presentation. More on that later.

FOOD HANDLING

<u>A word of caution is appropriate here.</u>

The handling of food is very important. It can be the petri dish in the kitchen. Food is full of bacteria - not all bad, but some of it is! Be sure to wash your hands and wash the food thoroughly as well as the surfaces on which you prepare the food. Chicken is especially dangerous, as raw chicken can contain salmonella germs that are very harmful to humans. The best advice I can give is to wash everything very well - surfaces, utensils, cooking equipment, and your hands. Also, pay attention to "use by" or "sell by" dates on food you buy.

The expression I've often used is "past the expiration date." But that was mostly in reference the ladies I was dating!

MISE EN PLACE: (Preparation of ingredients and dishes before cooking and serving). The way you prepare the ingredients is important to the final outcome of your meal. Do pay attention to good "prep." Many of the best chefs spend a lot of time in preparation of the food before they begin cooking it.

1) Wash everything well, for health concerns as well as appearance. Get rid of dirt, chemicals, bacteria, and handling by-products.

2) Cut, trim and peel.

<u>Cutting</u> will make it a *lot* easier to handle food. Also, be sure to cut away any blemishes, bruises, stems (if appropriate), and fat or bones in flesh (fish, meat, poultry) if it is not part of what should be cooked. In many cases, bones and some fat should be left intact in meat while cooking. But that will be detailed in each specific recipe.

Trimming is important, as many vegetables have root ends or stems that are tough to eat and not very visually appealing. For example, trim both ends of a carrot, onion, celery, and similar veggies. Mushrooms should be trimmed on the stem end, as that usually dries out when harvested. I personally use a lot of mushrooms, as they add a very distinct flavor to most foods.

Peeling is important for vegetables that have a hard or coarse skin. For example, I peel carrots, onions, squash, turnips, and the like. Sometimes I will peel potatoes, depending on how I am about to cook them. (This is described in detail with each recipe for potatoes).

3) Do measure properly! This is important, as the recipes are balanced regarding ingredients and flavor.

HEAT

Cooking is mostly about preparing, seasoning, and adding heat. Each recipe will suggest the appropriate seasoning, but let me tell you about the "heat" part.

There are basically two types of heat you can apply to food: dry heat or wet heat. A word of caution: Food likes to be put on/in the heat. Be sure to warm up your oven or pans before you try to cook the food. Don't put cold food in a cold pan or oven. Cold on or in cold does not work! The appropriate type of heat for each recipe is described in the directions for that recipe.

WET HEAT

Wet heat (moist) is heat conducted by water (including stock or sauces), or by steam.

Boiling: This is probably the most common type of cooking. It involves bringing a pot of water to a boil and then placing the food in the water. This method is used when you want to add water to the cooking food. If you are not using the water as a part of the food but still cooking it in boiling water, it is called poaching. Parboiling is like boiling, except the food only gets partially cooked and is usually finished by some other method of adding heat, like grilling.

Steaming: Very similar to boiling, except that the food is not placed directly in the boiling water. Rather, it is held above in the steam to cook.

DRY HEAT

Dry heat cooking is when the heat is conducted without moisture, i.e. by hot air, metal, radiation, or fat.

Grilling: We all know about the barbecue and grilling. It is considered "in" for the guys to be out in the yard in the summer grilling dinner. Grilling is putting the food on a grate or pan and placing it over an open flame, flipping it over to cook both sides.

Broiling: As in grilling, you are using an open heat source (flame) but are applying the heat from above rather than from below. As in grilling, you need to turn the food over and broil the other side to get an even cooking of the food.

Frying: This is cooking food in hot fat over moderate to high heat. If the food is completely submerged in the fat, it is called "deep frying." Pan frying is when you put only a small amount of fat in the pan and do not completely cover the food with the fat.

Roasting: This is the use of dry heat, but in a contained environment, such as an oven or covered pot. This method crisps the outside and leaves the inside tender but moist. I have roasted some piglets in the ground by digging a hole, making a fire in it, and then placing large rocks on the fire. I would leave the fire burning for many hours and then place the pig in the hole and cover it up. After about six hours, the pig's skin would be quite crisp and the meat inside would be very tender.

Baking: Like roasting, baking is the use of heat in an enclosed environment but usually with moist food and a lower temperature.

Sautéing: Add some fat (oil or butter) to a fry pan, heat, and then place the food in the hot fat. This is probably the easiest method of cooking. Be careful of the splashing fat when you add the food. This is usually done with a tight- fitting cover on the pan.

Braising: This is similar to sautéing except here you pan-fry the food first to brown the outside, and then you sauté it.

CHAPTER II

COURTING (FIRST IMPRESSIONS)

A LITTLE HOMEWORK!

Now that you are well stocked and can start thinking about preparing for a meal to entertain, there are a few basics that we should review.

MANdatory!

1) Always get a reading on any food biases that your intended guest (target) may have. For example, is she a vegetarian or even a vegan? Too bad if you prepared a beautiful lamb chop dinner and it turns out she does not eat meat. How about food allergies and special dietary restrictions? What a disaster if you make a wonderful Thai peanut sauce for your chicken and it turns out the lady is allergic to peanuts (a fairly common allergy). If you don't know this ahead of time, the evening could be a complete disaster. Also if you take the time to ask, you will surely make some points.

2) Be sure to clean, dust, and tidy up your abode before she arrives. Nothing is more of a turnoff than a messy place. For example, don't leave your bicycle in the dining room when trying to present her dinner. You may want to impress her about what a great jock you are, but leave that for conversation. Put all your athletic gear out of the way. Be sure to clean the kitchen. Women are impressed by guys who are neat and tidy. And of

course - clean the bathroom and be sure to have sufficient toilet paper in place. Your guest will inevitably visit it sometime during the evening - if only on her way to the bedroom. So be sure to make it presentable, like a clean mirror, clean towels, clean sink and toilet, clean floor, and be sure to check your medicine cabinet for presentability.

3) As a nice gesture, you should have an unopened new toothbrush in the medicine cabinet—just in case. Parenthetically, a lady friend of mine developed a product for the gals which she called "Just-in-Case." It was a small pouch that fit into a handbag and contained all the necessary late-evening and early-morning items like a toothbrush, condom, mouthwash, and other personal items that might come in handy if the occasion arose.

4) Don't leave any incriminating items around - like photos of old girlfriends, porn material, condoms, pharmaceutical or recreational drugs, dirty clothes, or workout clothing.

5) Turn off your answering machine. Who knows what calls you may receive during the evening, with an embarrassing message?

6) PUT THE TOILET SEAT DOWN!

7) Plan things well in advance! (Be optimistic!)

So far, so good. You have charmed this sweet damsel into coming to your roost and obviously gained her confidence enough to allow you the chance to entertain her.

TABLE SETTINGS

Knowing how to set the table correctly for dinner is important.

You should have a tablecloth, or at least place mats for each setting. Then, if possible, a charger would make a very nice touch – but it is not entirely necessary. Napkins (serviettes) are also important. You should then have glasses -a wine glass and a water glass -for each person.

Depending on how you will be serving the different courses of the meal, you may want to have the main dinner plates already on the table or ready in the kitchen to plate the food. A salad or soup bowl is also important. What I usually do is have the salad bowl or plate already on the table and serve the salad in a large bowl where your guest(s) can serve themselves. If you are plating the main course in the kitchen, then bring the food out already spread on the dinner plate.

Placing the cutlery in the proper way is also important. You should have two forks, a knife, and a spoon. Place the knife and spoon on the right and the forks on he left. You should put them in the order in which they will be used - salad fork, or smaller fork on the outside left, then the larger dinner fork inside. The spoon should be on the outside right and then the knife inside. Of course, you have the glass(s) to the upper right and the napkin folded nicely in the center of the cutlery.

A little trick I learned from a gourmet friend is if you holdup your hands and touch the tip of your thumb with the top of your index finger – your left hand forms the shape of a "b", that stands for bread. Hence the bread dish is on your left. The right hand forms the shape of a "d", that stands for drink. Hence the glasses go on your right.

And then the doorbell rings! The anticipated moment has arrived. Introduce her to any pets you may have, especially dogs. Cats will take their own sweet time to meet any strangers. Goldfish and birds - don't worry about them.

Obviously, you take her coat and hang it up.

At this point I usually say that the bar is open and pour an appropriate drink. (We will discuss drinks and alcoholic beverages in the following chapter.) Then I set out the hors d'oeuvres - either in the kitchen or in the living room. Hopefully you have done all the prep work for the meal and it is either cooked, being cooked, or is ready to be cooked. You should also have the table already set for the meal.

COOKING AND PRESENTATION

Try to have the food prepared ahead of time so that you are not so concentrated on the cooking that you ignore your guest. Sometimes, however, that is not possible, so pour her a nice drink - a glass of wine of the color of her choice, or mix a cocktail for her. Once she is reasonably comfortable, have her join you in the kitchen while you are doing the cooking. That will impress her.

Do not overcook the food; it will invariably tum to mush or get burned. Also try not to splash the cooking liquids all around.

Visual appeal is very important! Obviously, this is part of the reason you invited her over.

When ready to plate, first of all separate the different food groups you are serving. By that I mean, if you are serving vegetables along with meat or fish, do not slop them together. Put each in its own part of the dish. Then be sure you have the potatoes all together. Do not dripped any liquids or food along the side of the plate. If some does end up there, and inevitably some will, wipe it off with the edge of a clean dish towel. Be sure your plates are the appropriate size for the amount of food you are serving. Too much food on a plate is not very attractive, nor is too little.

When entertaining a date, you do not have to try and prove you are the best or greatest cook ever. What you really need to do is show you are reasonably competent and that you are making an effort. Females like to know that the guy is trying to do something for them. Competency and effort go hand in hand. One without the other, and you flunk out!

Be sure to have a small variety of food to serve - not just a plate of potatoes. If it is just hors d'oeuvres, then have at least a couple out. If it is a main course, have some veggies, starch (potatoes, pasta, etc.) and meat or fish. I once heard it said that if a fellow can cook a vegetable, starch, and protein and have them look nice and taste good, that is the "dateable trifecta." Dessert can be a solo.

Here are some hints on presentation:

- When putting the food on a plate, be sure the plate is the appropriate size for the amount of food -not too big, not too small but the "Goldilocks" size.

- Do not slop the food onto the plate. Try to keep each type separate. (One of the more impressive ways to present your masterpiece is to stack it on the plate, i.e. go vertical if appropriate.)

- Try to put some "decor" on the plate. By that, I mean, drizzle a little olive oil or some other appropriate sauce around the edges of the food. I know you 've seen it done in the finer dining restaurants.

Remember—failure is relative and is like contact lenses; it is in the eyes of the beholder. If the meal does not turn out quite the way you expected (read: disaster) there is always the next plan. You can either have another pitcher of martinis, call the local food delivery store, or exit laughing. What the ladies really appreciate is the fact that you have made an effort on their behalf.

PREPARATION

Obviously, you will need plates and cutlery as well as a few other basics in order to properly present your masterpieces. Visual appeal and presentation are very important in serving a meal.

Four each of the following:

- Plates: Dinner plates and side plates (salad, bread and/or dessert) Small bowls: Can be used for soup, salad, and cereal
- Spoons, knives, and forks
- Napkins
- Wine glasses
- Water glasses
- Place mats or tablecloth
- Serving platters
- Serving spoons
- Candles and music (very important for mood)

Don't forget the table and chairs!!!

One of the most important things you can do—not only to impress your lady friend but also to help make your life easier—is to clean as you go!

Real men can clean up and tidy up!

When you are finished with a pot or pan, put it in the sink with a little dish soap and hot water. This will loosen all the cooked-on particles of food and make it so much easier to clean later. Also, I usually keep a medium-sized mixing bowl in the sink with some soapy water in it and put the cooking utensils in it when I am done with them. This soaking helps with cleaning later on.

Another important point about clean as you go is to be sure to clean the surfaces of the cutting boards and/or the countertops as you use them. All it takes is a squeezed-out sponge to wipe down the surfaces. I usually cook with a dish towel slung over my shoulder and use this a lot to dry my hands and the surfaces after I have sponged them down. Don't make a huge mess and leave it stacked on the kitchen counter. This is a doubly bad sign. First it implies to your lady friend that you expect her to clean up for you, and secondly it shows her that you are really not a "neat" guy. If you leave a mess like this—what is the rest of your life like!

BONNE CHANCE AND BON APPÉTIT

CHAPTER III

FOREPLAY

(Alcoholic Beverages)

As I mentioned earlier in the introduction, this is not a book about alcohol, but I think it is important for a fellow to have a little knowledge about the subject. It will certainly help increase your odds of "success"! As the saying goes: "Candy is dandy, but liquor is quicker." So what I want to do in this chapter is to give you some of the basics and then let you expand from there.

WINE

First, let's discuss wines. This is one of the most misunderstood types of beverages because of all the mystique and hoopla associated with it. (I think a big part of the image about wine is still promoted by the wine industry.) Here a little knowledge is not a dangerous thing, but you do not need to know if 1996 was a wonderful year or that the wine has hints of raspberry with soft touches of honey and peaches. Wine can be made from a variety of fruits and other exotic plants such as dandelion flowers, strawberries, etc. But for our purposes we are going to focus on grape wine—which is the fruit used for 99.9% of all wines. When people refer to wine, they almost always mean wine made from grapes.

There is a certain protocol when serving wine. First, when storing wine, it should be kept at a cool temperature of around 50°-54° F. When ready to serve, let red wine warm up to room temperature before serving, but keep the white and sparkling wines cool. In the case of red wine, try to have the bottle opened about an hour—or at least half an hour—before you pour it. This gives the wine a chance to "breathe." That means letting the wine aerate, which will help soften the acidic and tannin tastes a bit. With white wine, you do not have to open the bottle a long time beforehand to let it aerate. White wine usually does not have as much acidity as red does. Also, with the coolness of white wine, you experience less of an acidic sensation on your tongue.

Next, when opening a bottle of any type of wine, examine the cork. You don't really need to smell the cork, as it will inevitably smell like cork! What you should do is look at the condition of the cork. Is it soft and spongy, or does it have red streaks running up the side? These symptoms are usually the first hint of a wine that has gone bad. Next, roll the cork lightly between your thumb and forefinger. Is it dry and flaky? This could also be a hint that the wine has "turned." Then take a little taste to make sure it tastes good. If it tastes sour or vinegary, it has gone bad. Pour it out and try a different bottle. Many wines now come with "screw tops" so you do not have to worry about the cork issue.

As an aside, there is a continuing debate regarding which is a better stopper for wine - cork or metal screw top. Both sides have their pros and cons. The issue is a little beyond this introduction to wines.

There are two basic types of wine - red and white. There is also rosé, or blush wine, but that is really a hybrid of red and white wine. All the juice that is squeezed out of grapes, be they red grapes or green grapes, comes out yellow. To make it into a red wine, the juice is allowed to soak in the red grape skins for up to a couple of weeks. (To make it a rosé wine, the juice soaks with skins of the red grapes for maybe a day or so.) If the wine is to be a white wine, it does not soak with the skins of any grapes. Then the juice is allowed to ferment - which is the yeast eating the natural sugar - thus creating the alcohol content. So we now have red or white wine!

In addition to these two major types of wines (rosé is a hybrid or these) aka table wines (sparkling wine is made from both) there are also some wines which are mostly "enhanced" (that is, a distilled spirit, such as brandy, is added to "fortify" the wine). These are called aperitifs and /or dessert wines. Examples of these are port, sherry, madeira, vermouth, and marsala. Other dessert wines include late- harvest rieslings, and/or "ice wine." You may prefer a liqueur, such as Cointreau or Frangelico, for after dinner.

Which wine to choose! There used to be the rule of thumb about red wine with heavier entrees like red meat, and white wine with lighter main courses like fish or poultry. Other than in the extreme situations like big cuts of beef or very light and flaky pieces of fish, these rules have broken down considerably.

Now it is certainly appropriate to serve either type of wine with whatever you are offering for the main course. For example, I recently had the pleasure of enjoying abalone as an appetizer this past Thanksgiving with a group of friends at my house. The person who brought the abalone is also a serious wine aficionado.

His choice of wine to accommodate the most tender and delicious abalone was pinot noir. What a surprise combination and sensory delight.

Let me go one step further and explain the main different kinds of grapes (called varietals) that are used for wine making, as opposed to table grapes that are eaten as a fruit.

In the red corner, we have the heavy weight of cabernet sauvignon. This is probably Napa's most successful wine. It is from the grape that makes the great red Bordeaux of France. This "varietal" improves with age (drink from 5 -10 years old to be safe). From there the next would be merlot, a smooth wine which is just a little lighter than the cabernet! Zinfandel is a particular California grape which makes a pleasant wine and is often mixed with green grapes to make a rosé. Next on my list of descending "body" would be a Syrah for which the Australian imports are noted. And then pinot noir (red Burgundy) in descending order of heaviness. There are of course many other varieties of grapes used to make wine, but to describe them would be more technical than you need to know at this point. My favorite, by the way, is pinot noir. It is a safe choice for almost any meal and can be reasonably priced. Oregon, California, and the Burgundy area of France produce some of the finest pinots, as does the Sonoma area of California. If you had the pleasure of seeing the movie *Sideways*, you know that great pinots also come from the Santa Barbara, California area. (A fun movie!)

White wines are a lighter type of wine and are very popular with the ladies as a before-dinner drink and also with the meal. Chardonnay is currently the most popular of the whites but also very pleasant are sauvignon blanc, pinot grigio, and Riesling.

Another type of white wine that always impresses the ladies is Champagne or some kind of a sparkling wine such as prosecco, or cava. Only wines from the Champagne area of France and made in the authentic style of double fermentation can properly be called Champagne. I think Champagne has a rather inflated image for the value. However, whatever works! Prosecco is a sparkling wine from Italy, Cava is the same, but from Spain and the Germans call theirs Sekt. The varieties of grapes that go into making each of these respective styles of sparkling wine differ depending on the country of origin.

Do not chill red wines, but do chill white and sparkling wines.

There are a lot of very interesting drinks that can be made with wines, e.g. sangria, Champagne cocktails, mimosas, Bob's Bubbly Pushover and wine spritzers, for all of which I will include a few recipes.

COCKTAILS: (VERY FREUDIAN TERM: THINK ABOUT ROOT STRUCTURE!).

It is a good idea to purchase a variety of cocktail glasses. For a start, I would suggest:

- Martini glasses,
- Highball glasses,

- Rocks glasses (also called Old-Fashioned glasses)
- Wine glasses.

In addition, a well-stocked home bar should have the following:

- A jigger glass -for measuring amounts to pour 1and 2 oz)
- A corkscrew/ bottle opener
- Cocktail shaker

One can serve the liquor straight—i.e. not mixed with anything but perhaps a little ice and/or water—or use it as a base for making a more elaborate type of drink.

In mixing cocktails, remember a "jigger" is 1oz, and a "dash" is 3 drops.

A well-stocked home bar should include some/or all of the following basic types of alcohol:

- Gin
- Vodka
- Scotch
- Rum
- Bourbon
- Tequila
- Triple Sec
- Vermouth (dry)
- White wine
- Red wine
- Sparkling wine (Champagne, prosecco, etc.)

And there are a few others that will be mentioned in the recipes for the specific cocktails.

HERE ARE SOME OF THE MOST POPULAR COCKTAILS FOR THE LADIES:

MAY I OFFER YOU A STIFF ONE?

All these are made with the astute advice of my favorite bartender "Mary" (retired) from the Pioneer Saloon.

MARTINI

> *One Martini is alright*
> *Two are too many, and*
> *Three are not enough!*
>
> James Thurber

The Classic Martini

INGREDIENTS:

4 jiggers gin   1 lemon
1 jigger dry vermouth

PREPARATION:
- Fill a cocktail shaker with ice,
- Pour in the gin and vermouth,
- Shake or stir vigorously.
- Pour into a martini glass and add a slice of lemon or an olive.

Or you can serve with a cocktail onion and then the drink is technically called a "Gibson."

Variations on the martini: These are fun and effective.

Bikini Martini

No more tan lines!

1 jigger each of pineapple and   1 jigger of pineapple juice
   coconut-flavored rum

- Pour over ice in a martini glass and serve.

Chocolate Kiss Martini

Even on the first date: Quite sweet.

1 jigger vodka   1 jigger white crème de cacao
1 jigger chocolate liqueur

- Serve chilled with drops of chocolate on top.

French Martini

Well, I don't think I need to make a comment

1 jigger vodka
1 jigger pineapple juice

1 jigger Chambord
(a French liqueur)

— Serve over ice.

Carol's Cosmopolitan

(Makes 4 drinks - 'cause you can't have just one)

1 cup vodka
1 cup cranberry juice
Juice of 1 freshly squeezed lime

1 cup Triple Sec or other orange
liqueur

— Pour all ingredients into a cocktail shaker filled with ice.
— Shake vigorously and pour into martini glasses
— Place one thin slice of the lime on the glass rim for decoration.

Manhattan

(Makes two drinks)

2 jiggers bourbon
1 jigger sweet vermouth

2 dashes bitters (6 drops) with a
maraschino cherry.

— Stir and serve over ice.

Margarita

(Makes two drinks)

2 jigger good quality tequila
2 jigger lemon or lime juice
  (preferably freshly squeezed)
1 lemon or lime wedge

1 jigger orange liqueur (such as
  Triple Sec or Cointreau)
A saucer with about ¼" salt
Ice

- Rub the lemon or lime wedge around the rim of two martini or rocks glass.
- Dip the rim of the glass into the salt and rotate until the right amount of salt has collected on the glass.
- Pour the tequila, juice, and orange liqueur into a shaker filled with ice. Give it a good shake.
- Pour into the salt-rimmed glass. Some like ice in the drink, others prefer no ice.

Daiquiri

(Makes two drinks)

2 jiggers light rum
Juice of ½ lime

1 tsp sugar

- Shake with ice. Pour into martini glasses.

Champagne Cocktail

ALWAYS A LADY'S FAVORITE!

1 sugar cube per drink
1 dash bitters splashed onto the
  sugar cube

1 bottle Champagne or
  sparkling wine

- Put the bitters infused sugar cube in the bottom of a champagne flute or white wine glass.
- Fill with Champagne. Enjoy!
- A variation of this drink is what I call "Cupid's Kiss" Instead of adding the cube of sugar and bitters, pour in about ½ oz of cassis

The Morning After Mimosa

(As Waylon and Willie sing: "For all the Girls I've Loved Before")

2 champagne flutes or white wine glasses

1 jigger orange juice in each glass

- Fill with Champagne
- A very refreshing way to start the day and restart the romance.

Bloody Mary

1 jigger vodka,
2 oz tomato juice
Juice of ½ lemon
Dash of salt
Dash of Tabasco
Dash of Worcestershire sauce
Pinch of horseradish

- Mix all together, shake over cracked ice, and pour into a highball glass.

Lizze's Elastic Melter

1 jigger tequila

1/3 oz crème de cassis

Juice of ½ lime

Ginger Ale

- Pour all ingredients into a tall glass with ice.

Billy's Candy: El Matador

1 jigger Tequila

2 jiggers pineapple juice

½ jigger lime juice

- Stir with ice and pour.

I promised you the recipe for...

"Bob's Bubbly Pushover"

A sangria punch to serve at a gathering of at least 6 friends.

1 bottle of rosé sparkling wine

2 cups pomegranate juice

2 cups orange juice

- Mix all ingredients in a large punch bowl with lots of ice, and pour into wine glasses.

CHAPTER IV
T & A (TAPAS & APPETIZERS)

I Refer to Them as "Appeteasers" aka: Hors d'oeuvres

Tapas-the Spanish form of appetizers and in our vernacular - appetizers. Hors d'oeuvres (which is the French word for appetizers) are a very important part of starting the evening right.

Tapas originally got the name from the Spanish verb "tapar," which means to cover. It all started when innkeepers would serve the weary travelers a glass of wine with a slice of bread over the glass to keep the flying critters out of the wine, provide a snack, and encourage the order of another glass of wine.

Appetizers set the mood for early libations and light chit-chat. With the proper hors d'oeuvres you can set the tone for the whole relationship - be it just the evening, or in my case, the rest of my life. Even though I had met my future wife on a number of common social occasions, it was when I was preparing some cucumber, smoked salmon, wasabi, and chive hors d'oeuvres that she was actually attracted to me. My story is, at a party at my house which she was attending with her then boyfriend, she tried some of these little bad boys and saw I was making more, so she sidled up to me, having put super glue on her shoulder, leaned against me and said, "Show me how you make these big, boy." Her story is somewhat different but for the sake of this book, I like mine better. (The recipe for this "successful" dish is included below.)

I categorize appetizers into cold and hot (no relationship to spices or partner's temperature and heavy breathing). Cold T & A's are those not requiring any cooking or heat. Obviously, hot ones do! As you know, heating things up requires some effort. But it is usually worth it!

COLD APPETIZERS

No preparation:

- Peanuts, served in a bowl.

- Olives—many varieties here, but pitted are the more appropriate type to serve along with a toothpick for selecting them out of the dish.

- A variety of cheeses, along with some crackers or slices of bread and a knife for serving.

- Chips and dip—many types of good dips are available at almost all grocery and convenience stores. One of my favorites is hummus.

- Tortilla chips and guacamole dip (available commercially).

- Marinated whole mushrooms (available in most supermarkets in cans or bottles).

- Cut veggies with dip, available already prepared at most supermarkets.

- Pre-cooked shrimp with cocktail sauce (available at most supermarkets.)

All the above can all be easily put out on plates and served as finger food.

Faux Caviar

1can black olives (chopped)	1/2 clove finely chopped garlic
1 tbsp olive oil	(be sure your date eats some too!)

– Mix all ingredients together and use as a spread on crackers.

Cherry Tomatoes Stuffed with Herb-Spiced Cheese

12 cherry tomatoes	Salt and pepper
1 package spiced goat cheese	

– Cut about 25% off the top of the tomatoes, scoop out the seeds and moisture
– stuff the hollowed-out tomatoes with the cheese, and place on a serving platter.
– Salt and pepper to taste.

Endive Lettuce Scoops with Smoked Salmon Cheese

2 heads of endive lettuce	cheese mixture
1 package smoked salmon	

– Cut the base stem off the lettuce, separate the leaves and wash in cold water
– spread a small scoop of the cheese onto the lettuce shells, and serve.

Melon Wrapped in Lox (Smoked Salmon)

Easy. Serves 4

1/2 melon of choice (not watermelon).

1 4oz package smoked salmon
2 wedges of lemon or lime

- Cut the melon into wedges.
- Wrap each wedge with a thin slice of salmon.
- Serve on a platter with the citrus wedges.

HOT APPETIZERS

These require some cooking time but make very special little nibbles. I think it is well worth the effort for that "special" someone.

Artichoke/Parmesan Cheese Dip

Very easy. Serves at least 4 with some left over.

1 jar (4 oz) artichoke hearts (drained)

½ cup Parmesan cheese
½ cup mayonnaise

- Combine all ingredients with a blender until smooth. Pour into an ovenproof shallow dish and bake in a 350° oven for about 10 minutes.
- Serve warm. However, I also like it at room temperature.
- Have guest spread on crackers or thin slices of toasted bread cut into 2" X 2" squares.

A very good variation on this is to use a can of tuna fish instead of the artichokes, and use only a tablespoon of mayo.

FRIED ONION SHREDS

Serves 2-4. Medium difficulty.

1 medium onion
3/4 cup flour

2 cups vegetable oil

- Slice the onion very thinly. Separate the slices into rings.
- Put the flour in a plastic baggie along with the onion rings; shake well to coat the onion rings.
- Put enough oil into a small frying or sauté pan and heat until a drop of water sizzles.
- Slowly and carefully place a few of the flour- coated onion rings at a time into the heated oil. They will fry very quickly.
- Remove the onion ring, drain on a paper towel and repeat the process until all rings are fried.
- Serve while still warm.

FRIED OYSTERS

This is my friend Ned's favorite appetizer recipe. Whenever he comes over I impose on him to make this. Easy (with some attention required) Serves - as many as the size jar of oysters you buy. Can be small, medium or large.

1 jar raw oysters (size depends on how many you want to make). A small jar for just the two or four
1 egg

6 - 12 saltine crackers—depends on how many you want to make.
3 tbsp vegetable oil

- Heat the oil in a frying or sauté pan over medium heat. Beat the egg with a little bit of water.

- Crush the crackers in a small plastic food storage bag. Pour the crushed crackers onto a plate.
- Dip the oysters into the egg wash and then into the crackers to coat.
- Place the oysters into the heated oil and fry on all sides. Drain on a paper towel and serve warm.

TEMPURA CAULIFLOWER

Easy and very impressive. Serves 4.

1 head cauliflower, cut into bite-sized flowerets

1 cup beer

1 cup all-purpose flour

2 cups vegetable oil for deep frying

Salt to taste

- Combine the flour and beer and let stand for about one hour.
- Preheat oil in sauce pan on medium heat.
- Coat the cauliflower flowerets in the beer/flour mixture Drop a few florets at a time into the heated oil until golden.
- Remove and drain on paper towels. Repeat until all the cauliflower is fried.

Shrimp with Cocktail Sauce

Very easy. Serves 4.

1 lb medium-sized frozen or fresh cooked shrimp, peeled but tail on.

1 small jar cocktail sauce.

- Boil a pot of water.
- Put shrimp into the boiling water and cook until they turn pink.
- Remove shrimp from water and put into a bowl of cold water.
- When the shrimp have cooled, serve on a plate with a bowl of the cocktail sauce.
- Have a small empty bowl alongside for the tails.

Puff Pastry Roll-ups

1 sheet puff pastry
Crumbly goat cheese

Sun-dried tomatoes

- Thaw sheet of puff pastry.
- Unfold and spread out on a cutting board. Sprinkle some crumbled goat cheese over the pastry.
- Sprinkle some dried tomatoes over the cheese. Roll up the pastry to a cigar shape.
- Cut the roll crossways into ½-inch slices.
- Put on a baking sheet and place in a 400° oven for about 10 minutes or until lightly browned.
- Serve either warm or cold.

CHAPTER V

S & M
(SOUPS, SALADS, SANDWICHES, AND MORE)

When you are on the run or pressed for time, nothing fills the bill better than a "quickie." Soups and salads are great, as are sandwiches. They are easy to make and heat up quickly (some like it hot). There is the hearty style, open face, and as with salads, they can even be served dressed or undressed. The choices are yours, as there is lots of variety. And we all know that variety is the spice of life.

SOUPS

Soup is one of the easiest and most heart-warming ways to start a meal. I like to break the kinds of soups down into those that are warm (temperature) and those that are cold. A nice warm soup on a blustery autumn or winter day (evening) is always a welcome course to serve. And on a warm summer evening, a cold soup really hits the spot.

Salad is probably one of the easiest courses to make. However, it can also be one of the more difficult - depending on how elaborate you want it to be. I personally try to keep my salads pretty simple.

Sandwiches are one of the basic foods, I think. For as long as I can remember I have been eating sandwiches. They make a very nice complement to a bowl of soup or a salad.

FRENCH ONION SOUP

Easy. Serves 4.

This is one of my favorites and easy to make. It has a great WOW value!

Here is my favorite story about this French onion soup. One summer my future mother-in-law was staying with us for a couple of weeks, and one evening I made this recipe. Well, I knew I had her approval to marry her daughter as soon as she tasted it. She could not stop talking about how good it was and that she wanted it every night for dinner. This was coming from a lady who hardly ate anything.

INGREDIENTS:

1 medium-sized onion,
   quartered and thinly sliced
2 cans beef broth
1 tbsp butter 1 tbsp flour

1 cup water
½ cup Monterey jack cheese,
   grated
1 slice French bread per person.

DIRECTIONS:

- Preheat oven to 400°
- Sauté the onion slices in the butter in a medium-sized pan for about 15 to 20 minutes, until soft and translucent.
- Stir in the flour and slowly add the water and broth. Bring to a boil and then turn down the heat to a simmer. Cook for about another 20 minutes.
- While the soup is cooking, toast the bread.
- When the soup is cooked, pour into the serving bowls, place a slice of the toast on top of the soup, and sprinkle the grated cheese over the toast.

- Place in the oven to bake until the cheese is melted -about 10 minutes.
- Serve immediately.

Having lived in Canada for many years, I have a Canadian version of the French onion soup which is really very good and easy to make.

Canadien French Onion Soup

Aye! Very easy,

Serves 4, (Not a spelling error. That is the way the French Canadiens spell the word, as in the name of the hockey team from Montreal.)

INGREDIENTS:

1 quart beef broth

1 large onion, quartered and sliced

1 cup heavy cream

½ cup all-purpose flour

1 cup cheddar cheese, shredded

½ cup croutons

Salt and pepper to taste

DIRECTIONS:
- In a medium-sized pot, bring the broth to a boil, Stir in the onion slices and reduce heat to a simmer. Let the onions cook for about 15 minutes.
- Stir in the flour slowly, making sure it does not lump, and bring the mixture back to a simmer. Pour in the cream and cheese.
- Stir and cook until the cheese melts.
- Put into the serving bowls and sprinkle a few croutons on top.

Beer Cheese Soup

Easy. Serves 4.

Another of my favorites, having spent many years in Vermont and enjoyed this soup on many an evening with my friends. After we finished cross-country skiing we would return to my place for a warm, cozy dinner by the fireside, and this soup would be either the first course or the main course along with a salad.

INGREDIENTS:

1 bottle beer	½ onion, minced
½ cup Cheddar cheese, shredded	1 tbsp butter
	1 clove garlic, minced
1 cup half-and-half	1 tbsp Worcestershire sauce
2 cups chicken broth	¼ cup flour

DIRECTIONS:

- In a medium-sized pot, bring the broth to a boil, Stir in the onion slices and reduce heat to a simmer.
- Let the onions cook for about 15 minutes.
- Stir in the flour slowly, making sure it does not lump, and bring the mixture back to a simmer.
- Pour in the cream and cheese.
- Stir and cook until the cheese melts.
- Put into the serving bowls and sprinkle a few croutons on top.

Red Pepper Soup

Easy. Serves 4.

One evening not too long ago, my sister and her husband came over for dinner. I made this red pepper soup as a starting course. As I was cooking the soup, my sister asked what kind it was. When I told her she said not to tell her husband, as he does not like red peppers. So, we said it was tomato soup. He proceeded to eat it and exclaimed that it was the best tomato soup he has ever had.

INGREDIENTS:

4 red bell peppers, cored and
   diced
1 quart chicken broth
1 onion, diced

2 cloves garlic, chopped
1 tbsp butter
1 cup cream
Salt and pepper to taste

DIRECTIONS:

- Sauté the red peppers, onion, and garlic in the butter until soft—about 6-7 minutes—in a sauce pan.
- Put in the chicken broth and let the mixture simmer for about 1 hour.
- Pour it all into a blender and purée. Be careful when blending hot liquids, as it could splash out of the blender jar and cause some discomfort to you and/or make a mess.
- Pour the puréed mixture back in the saucepan and add cream.
- Stir well and heat to a simmer. Serve and enjoy.

A GREAT PURÉED POTATO SOUP

Easy. Serves 4.

The wonderful thing about potato soup is that it can be served hot or cold. If served cold, it is called vichyssoise.

INGREDIENTS:

4 medium potatoes, peeled and
   cubed
½ onion, or 1 shallot, chopped
4 cups vegetable stock

2 tbsp butter
1 cup cream
Salt and pepper to taste

DIRECTIONS:

- In a medium-sized sauce pan melt the butter and then put the potatoes and onion (shallot) into the pan.
- Heat for about 3 minutes, then add the vegetable stock. Put the heat on simmer and let cook for about 1 hour. Pour mixture into a blender and purée.
- Return mixture to pot, stir in the cream, and reheat.

If you are making it into vichyssoise, no need to reheat.

Just put in the refrigerator to cool.

COLD SOUPS

By way of introduction to cold soups, the above puréed potato soup can be served cold as vichyssoise (see above).

My favorite and most spectacular cold soup is radish soup. Here is my very special recipe.

Chilled Radish Buttermilk Soup

Easy. Serves 4.

INGREDIENTS:

12 lbs trimmed radishes	1 teaspoon salt
3/4 lbs seedless cucumbers	1 teaspoon rice vinegar
2 cups (1pint) chilled buttermilk	½ teaspoon sugar

DIRECTIONS:

- Put all ingredients in a blender and purée.
- Garnish with 1 or 2 very thin slices of radish and cucumber.

Strawberry Soup

Very easy. Serves 4

INGREDIENTS:

2 pints strawberries	½ cup water
2 cups yogurt	1 pinch ground cardamom
½ cup orange juice	Directions:

- Combine everything in a blender and purée. Chill and serve. Garnish with half a strawberry.

Gazpacho

Easy. Serves 4.

One time when I was in Spain, we were in Seville and eating at a wonderful restaurant, which I called Alberto's. The gazpacho there was so fabulous that I asked the waiter for a second portion. As he was pouring me some more soup, I told him how wonderful it was. His reply was that if is not good in Seville it won't be good anywhere, as

Andalucía (the province in which Seville is located) is the home of gazpacho. Later, my Spanish-speaking girlfriend asked if I remembered the name of the restaurant. When I told her, she asked how I knew. Well, it was easy, as there was a sign in the window. She thought that was one of my funniest jokes. I didn't understand until she told me the sign really read "Abierto" - which means "open" in Spanish. In any case, here is their recipe.

INGREDIENTS:

2 cups tomato juice

½ onion, minced

½ cucumber, peeled and minced

½ green bell pepper, minced

1 can (8 oz) chopped tomatoes

1 clove garlic, minced

2 tbsp red wine vinegar

½ jar (4 oz) diced pimiento peppers

1 dash tabasco sauce

1 lemon, juiced

1 tbsp chopped chives

Salt and pepper to taste

1 cup croutons

DIRECTIONS:

- Combine all the ingredients except the chives and croutons in a blender and pulse until well mixed but still a bit chunky.
- Chill in refrigerator for about 2 hours.
- Pour into chilled bowls, top with the chives and croutons.

CHILI

(a form of soup)

One of the fun and easy meals to make for two, four, or a bunch of friends is chili. I remember having the whole rugby team over for a Super Bowl party, and the day before I started cooking up my chili. This was a hard task, as one of the players' wives was the food and beverage manager at the local high-end golf club. She always made great food for our after the game parties, - our Bar-B-Q picnics for ourselves and the visiting team. Anyway, I was about to rise to the occasion!

So my chili chore began. After interviewing many foodie friends, I finally settled on "Bob's Basic Chili Recipe," which I got from my friend and mentor Chef Lynn, who is one of the cutest chefs you could ever hope to meet. I have since renamed it and now refer to it as a Hawaiian Chili -just because of the name—ComeaWannaleiYa Chili. Just think of how much more chili the guys in the rugby club would have eaten if I called it that back then! I actually got the idea for the name from my friend Butch the sausage maker at the Monterey Farmers Market in California. His suggestion was "IMAWANNACOMALAYA"

Here is the basic recipe. It is vegetarian to start, but as you will see in the notes below, you can add many different meat ingredients for variety. Very quick, easy, tasty, filling, healthy, and not at all expensive.

ComeaWannaleiYa Chili

(serves 4)

1 tbsp olive oil
1 large onion -diced
1 red pepper-seeded and diced
1 tbsp minced garlic
1 tsp red chili pepper flakes
2 cups canned green lentils, drained

2 cups canned chopped tomatoes
2 cups canned red kidney beans, drained
½ tsp ground cumin
Salt and pepper to taste

- Heat the oil in a large sauce pan, then add the onions, garlic, red pepper, and chili pepper. Simmer for about 20 minutes, stirring occasionally. Add the balance of the ingredients and mix well. Let simmer for about another 10 minutes.
- To serve, place the chili in a bowl and top with grated cheese and/ or sour cream. You can also additionally top it with chopped parsley, avocado, and/or sliced scallions.

This is the basic vegetarian version -which is good by itself.

However, to change the type of chili you can add any of

- ½ lb ground beef or ½ lb ground turkey lightly sautéed
- ½ lb ground chicken -lightly sautéed
- ½-inch pieces cooked bacon

SALADS

(can be served dressed or undressed)

Salad are easy to make and can do so much to dress up a plate of food. However, my preference is to serve the salad in a small side bowl or dish. I do this because I like a lot of dressing on my salads. If I included it on the plate with the main course or even a sandwich, the dressing would run onto the other food, which I don't want.

Here are four easy salad recipes and some suggestions for dressing (the salad, that is). Also included is a simple recipe for coleslaw -which I really enjoy.

Chef Salad

Easy. Serves 4.

INGREDIENTS:

1 small bag of mixed greens (available in most grocery stores

4 slices oven-roasted turkey or chicken breast

½ cup cheddar cheese, shredded

½ cup Italian dressing l tomato, quartered

1 avocado or green pepper or artichoke hearts or almost any kind of fresh vegetable

2 hard-boiled eggs

DIRECTIONS:

– Wash the mixed greens in cold water and blot the excess water with a paper towel. Put in a large bowl.

– Slice the turkey (or chicken) breasts into strips and place on the greens.

– Sprinkle the shredded cheese over the mixture, add the dressing and toss the whole salad. Place the tomato wedges, other vegetables, and sliced eggs on top.

   Present to the table with a serving spoon and fork. Let each person serve themselves.

Tomatoes And Green Goddess Dressing

Very easy. Serves 4.

INGREDIENTS:

4 large tomatoes

½ cup Green Goddess dressing, available at grocery stores.

DIRECTIONS:

- Cut the tomatoes into either slices or wedges and place on a serving platter.
- Pour the dressing over the tomatoes. Sprinkle with salt and pepper to taste.
- Present the serving platter with serving utensils and let each person help themselves.

Iceberg Lettuce Wedges and Blue Cheese Dressing

Very easy. Serves 4.

INGREDIENTS:

1 head iceberg lettuce, cut into 4 wedges	**1 cup blue cheese dressing (I like a lot of dressing!)**

DIRECTIONS:

- Place one lettuce wedge on each plate.
- Pour over the amount of dressing you would like.
- Salt and pepper to taste.
- Serve!

Now is that easy, or what?

Chicken Caesar Salad

Easy. Serves 4.

This salad is not quite as easy to make as the previous ones, but it is more interesting and well worth the extra effort. It is very popular in restaurants and can be served as a side salad or as the main course.

INGREDIENTS:

(Double everything if using as a main course)

1 head Romaine lettuce	½ cup Caesar salad dressing
1 cooked chicken breast	1 cup Italian seasoned croutons
(skinned and boned)	½ cup grated Parmesan cheese

DIRECTIONS:

- Cook the chicken breast, if not already done, then cut into one-inch cubes.
- Chop up the Romaine lettuce. Discard the heavy white core, Place both the chicken and lettuce in a large bowl and toss with the dressing.
- Sprinkle the cheese and croutons on top and serve.

COLESLAW

Very easy. Serves 4.

I like coleslaw with almost any sandwich and with any barbeque meal, especially hamburgers.

INGREDIENTS:

½ head green or red cabbage	½ cup mayo
1 large carrot, peeled and grated	Juice of one freshly squeezed
1 tbsp fresh chives, chopped	lemon
½ cup buttermilk	

DIRECTIONS:

- Mix all ingredients in a bowl, salt and pepper to taste. Serve!

And now for my very favorite! Very easy. Serves 4. I have often made this salad as my main course, it is so good.

But be sure to get fresh, well-ripened tomatoes. I ordered this as an appetizer one evening, and the tomatoes were so hard and tasteless that I was moved to write an email to the management when I returned home. I told him that if the chef had not tasted the tomatoes before he served then, shame on him. But if he had tasted them and still served them, double shame!

The story behind the making and naming of this salad– a story I tend to believe -is that a food editor of the *New York Times* newspaper was visiting The Isle of Capri and had a very nice tomato and cheese salad with a splash of balsamic. When she returned home she made the salad and added a few basil leaves to give it the color of the Italian flag (red, white, and green) and she named it after the island: Caprese.

INGREDIENTS:

2 ripe heirloom tomatoes, thinly sliced

1 ball fresh mozzarella cheese, thinly sliced

¼ cup shredded basil leaves

1 tbsp balsamic vinegar

Salt and pepper to taste

DIRECTIONS:

- Spread the tomato slices around the dish. Put the slices of cheese on the tomatoes,
- Take a large pinch of the shredded basil leaves and place in the center of the plate.
- Splash the balsamic vinegar over the tomatoes. Salt and pepper to taste.

Now I will give you one quick and easy recipe for a salad dressing.

(Remember, the objective is "Undressing"!)

Easy Salad Vinaigrett

Vinaigrette is the basis for almost all salad dressings. Once you have this basic recipe down pat, you can add many different types of flavor. For example, if you want "blue cheese" dressing, just crumble a package of blue cheese in the vinaigrette.

Or perhaps you would prefer to serve honey-mustard dressing (one of my favorites). Then just add in a tablespoon of honey and an additional teaspoon of Dijon mustard.

The varieties are almost endless-it is up to your imagination!

Here is the basic recipe:

INGREDIENTS:
½ cup olive oil
½ cup red wine vinegar
½ tbsp Dijon mustard

½ tsp each of salt and pepper
Directions:

— Whisk all ingredients together.

SANDWICHES

When I was growing up - if I ever have! -sandwiches were such a basic part of our everyday diet. It was mostly a slice of Kraft cheese between two slices of white bread, or peanut butter and jelly spread on some old crusty plain bread. However, the sandwich has progressed so dramatically in our current diet that for me to try and describe all the variations would take me volumes. The best way for me to get ideas about sandwiches is to go to a restaurant and see what they are offering by way of fillings.

At this point I have a confession to make! I cannot go to New York City without having my NYC fix. It is a half corned beef, half pastrami, on rye bread with hot mustard. Now that is living! I was in Las Vegas for a meeting not too long ago and my host took me to one of the casino hotels that had a deli. Well the featured sandwich was a "Woody Allen Special." It was at least six inches high and absolutely stuffed with corned beef and pastrami. I didn't need to play at the gaming tables on that trip. I was already a winner just from the sandwich.

Sandwiches are great just by themselves or with a cup of soup or a salad. My favorite is the panini (an Italian- style toasted bread sandwich which is made on a grilling pan or a special toaster. I've invested in a panini toaster and use it constantly. The one drawback I find is that I am eating a lot more bread than I normally do.

For me to describe all the various types of sandwiches would be long and tedious - for both of us. So let me just give a few recipes of my favorite and easy to make ones.

Let's start with bread. It is important to choose a good bread. The plain old white sliced bread will not do. There is no taste and it won't hold up to the filling. Also crumbly bread or bread with a lot of holes in it will not work well. A very crusty bread will make the sandwich hard to eat.

You can have an open-face sandwich, which is just one slice of bread with a topping. For example:

Tuna Melt

Easy. Serves 4.

INGREDIENTS:

1 can albacore tuna

¼ cup mayonnaise

1 tbsp mustard

1 stalk washed celery, chopped

1 green onion (scallion) chopped

4 slices bread. Can be white or grain bread.

4 slices cheddar cheese

DIRECTIONS:

– With a fork, smash up the chunks of tuna. Place in a bowl with the chopped vegetables Stir in the mayo and mustard

– Mix well.

– Optional -toast the bread,

– Spread the tuna mixture on the bread,

– Place a slice of cheese on each and broil in the oven very briefly. Be careful: it will burn.

– Serve on a plate with potato chips or some other "munchies" snack.

Tortilla Wrap

Easy. Serves 4.

Wraps are a new form of one-sided sandwiches. They can be made with a great variety of fillings. All it takes is your imagination. For example:

INGREDIENTS:

4 – 8 grilled tortillas, about 10 inches in diameter, available at most grocery stores.

2 cups browned hamburger meat, or diced chicken, or

fish fillets. Use any kind of main ingredient that you feel comfortable with.

1 cup grated cheddar cheese

½ cup seasoning of your choice,

could be ketchup, or tartar sauce, or mayonnaise.

1 leaf of lettuce per wrap
1 slice of tomato per wrap

DIRECTIONS:
- Place each tortilla (one or two per person) on a flat surface and put ½ cup filling of your choice in each one.
- Spread the appropriate sauce over the filling. Sprinkle the grated cheese on each.
- Cover with a leaf of lettuce and a slice of tomato. Roll the wrap into a round hot dog shape.

Or you can make a sandwich with two slices of bread.

For example:

GRILLED CHEESE AND TOMATO SANDWICH

(plus variations):

INGREDIENTS:

2 slices of bread per sandwich
2 slice cheddar or other hard cheese per sandwich

1 tomato, thinly sliced
Butter
Salt and pepper to taste

DIRECTIONS:
- Butter the outside of the slices of bread.
- Place the cheese and tomato slices on the bread.
- Put the second slice of bread on the sandwich and grill, or fry in a pan.
- Many variations of this simple grilled sandwich can be made. For example, instead of the tomatoes, use raw or grilled onions. Ham and cheese is also a popular sandwich which is basically the same in preparation.

Other suggestions include:

- Crab meat and lettuce
- Grilled boneless chicken
- Scrambled eggs
- Leftover meatloaf
- Slices of steak
- Corned beef

And the list goes on!

I have not tried to be too detailed in describing or delineating many sandwich recipes, as the sandwich is so familiar to all of us.

THE GREAT B.L.T.

(Bacon, lettuce, and tomato)

Always an easy one to make. Sometimes I include a few wedges of avocado as well, which gives the sandwich a smoother and creamier texture.

INGREDIENTS:

2 slices of bread per sandwich (toasted)
1 or 2 leaves of lettuce
2 slices of tomato
4 slices of bacon

DIRECTIONS:

- Assemble all the ingredients on the bread. Place the two slices on top of each other. Cut the sandwich in half and enjoy.

Peanut Butter and Banana Sandwich

An easy and quick snack.

INGREDIENTS:

2 slices of bread per sandwich   1 banana

2 tbsp of peanut butter

DIRECTIONS:

—   Spread the peanut butter on the bread Slice the banana into ½-inch thick rounds Place the banana slices onto the peanut butter.

—   Fold the other piece of bread on top Cut in half and enjoy.

For some variety you can spread on strawberry jam instead of the banana.

CHAPTER VI

INTERCOURSE (THE PAUSE THAT REFRESHES)

W hat do you call it when you are between courses?
Intercourse
— of course!

Well, this is really not a chapter in a cookbook. Rather, it is some suggestions about taking a pause during your efforts to entertain your special guest.

It is important to take a break here and let the previous activities sink in as well as think ahead about what you need to be doing.

- Time to "digest" the previous conversation.

- Time to refill the wine or cocktails.

- Make sure the music is appropriate and still playing.

- Refill the water glasses.

- Pick up the used plates and/or soup or salad bowls.

- Make sure the appropriate cutlery is on the table for the next courses.

AND pay attention to your guest!

CHAPTER VII
THE MAIN EVENT - MEAT

Other than the initial presentation (visual appeal), the entrée, aka the Main Event, creates the greatest impression on your guest. It is important to get it right.

My friend Peggy, a TV comedy writer, uses the metaphor of serving the main course to a baseball game. Do you want to hit a "home run," or just a "single"? Either way, don't strike out! By this she means you can make a BIG impression or just a little one.

I have broken the chapter down into three main areas: Red Meat, Foul, and Seafood. Each category has a number of delicious recipes and most are fairly simple and easy.

One item that is important to have when cooking meat is a good instant meat thermometer. This will show you on the face the desired internal temperatures for various stages of cooking, depending on how well cooked you want it. A good thermometer will have indications for beef, veal, pork, and poultry. Insert the meat thermometer into the thickest part of the meat and watch to see what the temperature rises to. If there is a bone in the meat, be sure not to have the thermometer contact it, as it will give a false reading.

There is another way to tell how well cooked a piece of meat is, but it really takes some degree of expertise to do it properly. This other way is by pressing down on the meat and seeing how soft, or hard, it is.

Ideally if you touch the tip of your forefinger to the tip of your thumb and press the fatty part of your thumb that degree of softness equates to the meat being cooked "rare." Do the same with your middle finger and thumb; that softness is "medium." And then do it again with your ring finger - that equates to "well done."

A hint: Once you remove the meat from the heat, let it rest for about five minutes, as this will allow the meat to reabsorb some of its juices.

BEEF

Everyone's favorite (except the vegetarians): The All- American Special—Steak!

There are many ways to cook a good steak. You can grill, barbeque, fry, roast, or broil it. The difference between grilling and barbequing is the length of time. Technically grilling is done over high or medium heat with food that does not require long cooking times (under 20 minutes). Barbequing is done on lower heat and over a longer period of time. What we call barbequing today in the outdoors is really grilling. But who cares about the technical differences—we will use the words interchangeably - it is all good fun!

A further consideration, if you are going to barbeque (grill) steak is the type of seasoning to use. There are "rubs" and "marinades." Rubs are dry combinations of herbs and spices and should be added shortly before cooking. They add flavor, color, and a slight bit of protection for the tender meat from the heat and to help retain moisture. Marinades, on the other hand, are liquids, usually oil-based. They are meant to be applied to your food well in advance of cooking to give the meat a chance to absorb and be permeated by the seasoning. There is also barbeque sauce, which is best to put on the food near the end of cooking, as it contains sugar or molasses which burns at high heat. But it does allow a nice browning at the end of cooking.

Steak On The Grill

Serves two. Very easy.

We've all been there - craving a thick juicy steak!

INGREDIENTS:

2 8oz steaks: (cut at least 1½"
thick) Buy the best you can
afford. Make sure it has some
fat around it or through it.

Salt and pepper
1tbsp butter (herb-flavored if
desired)

DIRECTIONS:

- Prepare the grill and heat to medium (350°)
- Season the steaks with salt and pepper. Let stand 15 minutes.
- Grill over direct heat (about 8" above heat source) for 8 to 10 minutes (for medium rare, longer for more doneness) turning steaks one or twice.
- Remove steaks from the grill and let stand for about 5 minutes.

American Special—All Dressed Up

Serves 4

This recipe is similar to the Steak on the Grill, except it requires a few more ingredients and about 2 hours of marinating time. But it is well worth it. With a little planning ahead, you can have this all ready by the time Miss Lovely arrives. The recipe was given to me by my friend Dick in Vermont, who was a master at cooking up delicious twists on fairly standard fare.

INGREDIENTS:

2 lbs sirloin steak, cut 1½" thick
½ cup Kahlua liqueur
3 tsp lemon juice

1 tsp salt
½ tsp ground pepper

– Mix all the ingredients, except the steak, together.
– Place steak in a shallow dish or pan, pour the ingredients on top.
– Let marinate for 2 hours or longer (up to 6 hours) in refrigerator.
– Grill over medium heat for 8 minutes on each side for medium rare, longer for medium or well done.

Pepper Steak (Steak Au Poivre)

Serves two or four. Very easy.

When I was in academia, I spent a number of summers on the south coast of Spain under the guise of doing research. One year I was on the coast and rented an apartment right on the beach. There was a small (6 tables) restaurant just down the beach and all the locals would gather there each evening to see who could tell the best stories (the last liar standing won). The restaurant was run by a fellow named Jacques whom we all called affectionately "Creamy Jacques" because everything he cooked had cream in it. His background was very interesting, as he was a modern-day pirate. He had a small sailboat and during the winter month (off season for his cooking) he would load his boat up with buttons and sail to England, coming ashore in some remote part of Wales, thus circumventing the importation duties and tariffs. In any case, here is his recipe for steak au poivre, which is one of the easiest and best I have ever tasted. Jacques always cooked the meat in a frying pan.

INGREDIENTS:

2 or 4 filets mignons (each about 6 oz and 2" thick)
1 tbsp butter
1 tbsp crushed peppercorns
2 shallots, thinly sliced

½ cup heavy cream
½ cup brandy (optional)

DIRECTIONS:

- Melt the butter in a skillet over medium heat. Lightly salt and pepper the steaks then put in skillet.
- Cook for about 5 minutes on each side for medium rare Remove steaks, sauté the shallots in the juice left by the steaks until lightly browned (2-3 minutes).
- Put in the cracked peppercorns, the cream, and the brandy, stirring constantly until heated but not boiling (2-3 minutes). Plate the steaks and pour the cream sauce over them.

ROASTS

When someone speaks of roasts, there are basically two types - rib roast and pot roast. Prime rib is cooked with dry heat, and roasted in the oven; pot roast is cooked in a pot with a lot of liquid like water, stock, and/or wine. I used to use bourbon whiskey in place of wine.

Prime rib is easy, as all you do is buy a 2-3 rib roast, rub with powdered garlic and salt, put in a preheated 350° oven for 1 ½ hours. Take it out, let it rest about 15 minutes, carve, and serve. Serves 4 with leftovers.

Pot roast requires a little more prep and longer cooking time as you use lower heat.

Serves 4

INGREDIENTS:

2-3 lbs rump or chuck roast, tied (the butcher will do this for you)
2 onions, chopped
1 garlic glove, sliced

1 cup red wine (or bourbon)
1 cup beef broth
1 cup water
1 tbsp olive oil

- Put the olive oil in a large roasting pot with a tightly fitting lid.
- Heat the pot over low heat and put in all the ingredients Cook for about 3 hours, adding some water as necessary to keep the meat moist. If it is drying out, the heat is too high.
- Pierce the meat with a long fork When it is tender, it is done.
- Remove from pot and let cool for 10 minutes.
- While the meat is cooling, turn the heat up and reduce the juices to athick gravy.
- Carve the roast, plate, and pour on the gravy.

Great to serve with mashed potatoes.

VEAL

VEAL SCALLOPINI

Serves 4. Quick and Easy.

Veal is very young beef that has been in restricted quarters for about 6-9 months and fed mostly milk. It is very tender and cooks easily. I always enjoy cooking this as it can be done in less than 15 minutes.

INGREDIENTS:

1 lb veal, sliced ¼" thick. (Your butcher will slice it for you)
1 cup dry white wine
½ cup all-purpose flour
1 lemon, one half squeezed for
juice, other half thinly sliced
4 tbsp butter (½ stick)
1 tbsp capers, drained
Salt and pepper

DIRECTIONS:

Heat a large skillet and then melt the butter in it.

Dredge the pieces of veal in a flour, salt and pepper mixture. Cook the veal in the skillet on one side for about 2 minutes. Turn the veal over, add the lemon juice, wine, and capers.

Cook for 2 more minutes, plate, and add the lemon slices.

Hamburger (And Variations): The All-American Meal

INGREDIENTS:

1 lb ground beef   Salt and pepper
4 hamburger buns

DIRECTIONS:

- Divide the meat into four equal portions.
- Roll each portion into 4" patties and make a small indentation in the top of each with your thumb.
- Either grill or fry the patties for about 2 minutes per side.
- While the meat is cooking, grill or fry the tops and bottoms of each bun. Be careful not to burn the bread!
- Place the cooked patties on the bottom part of the buns Add whatever sauces or toppings you wish, i.e. ketchup, mustard, relish, and mayonnaise.

Now comes the time to get creative!

To make it into a cheeseburger you should add the slices of cheese to each patty as you are cooking the second side.

To make a bacon burger, add the slices of cooked bacon to the patties once you have placed them on the buns.

To make a mushroom burger, sauté the mushrooms in olive oil until dark brown. Place on the patties.

To make a mushroom, cheese, and bacon burger just add all the ingredients to the patties on the bun.

BURGUNDY BEEF (BEEF IN WINE, OR BOEUF BOURGUIGNON)

Serves 4+ This dish is very good as leftovers and reheated). In fact, one time a group of buddies and I went houseboating on Lake Powell with our respective dates or wives. We were each supposed to take a dinner entrée, so I made a big batch of Burgundy Beef, froze it, and took it on the trip. In all due modesty, I must say it was a spectacular hit.

This is the king of beef stews, and very simple.

You can add a great variety of other ingredients, and the simmering can take place either on top of the stove or in the oven.

INGREDIENTS:

1½ lbs chuck roast, cut into 1" cubes	2 tsp bottled brown gravy sauce
2 tbsp butter	2 cups water
¼ cup sherry	2 cups red wine (Burgundy)
½ lb mushrooms, quartered	1 bay leaf
6 tbsp flour	1 tsp mixture of thyme, sage,
2 tsp ketchup	and rosemary (seasoning)
	1 lb pearl onions, peeled

DIRECTIONS:

- Brown the beef in butter. Pour sherry over the beef, then remove with slotted spoon.
- Add mushrooms to pan, cook for one minute.
- Stir in flour, ketchup, gravy sauce, and water.
- Cook, stirring until mixture begins to boil.
- Return meat to pan and add 1 cup wine and remaining seasoning, including the bay leaf.
- Place onions on top of meat
- Cover pan and simmer 2 to 2 ½ hours, until meat is tender, adding the rest of the wine as needed
- A batch of mashed potatoes or crusty French bread to absorb the extra gravy is a must.

MEATLOAF

Here is another suggestion for a "quickie." Meatloaf is usually a time-consumer regarding preparation and cooking time. However, here is a recipe that will take you about 30 minutes in total. I love meatloaf and in fact have had a number of "cook-offs" regarding meatloaf. It is also very good as a leftover, either cold or reheated. Great as a leftover sandwich with some ketchup! My favorite recipe is included as "Joe's" most popular request along with a few variations of this most popular dish.

GRILLED MEATLOAF

Serves 4. Cook time: 10minutes. Total time-30 min.

INGREDIENTS:

4 tbsp olive oil	1 egg
(3 separated and 1)	½ cup ketchup
½ cup bread crumbs	2 tbsp grated parmigiano cheese
8 basil leaves, chopped	¼ lb grated mozzarella cheese
4 green onions chopped	Salt and pepper to taste.
1lb ground beef	

- Mix 1tbsp olive oil and all the other ingredients, except the mozzarella cheese, in a large mixing bowl. Mix well. Shape the mixture into a couple of loafs and rub with the remaining olive oil. Make a seam down the middle of the loafs and insert the mozzarella cheese, cover with meat. Place on the grill and make a quarter turn every couple of minutes, when each side becomes well grilled. Should take about 10min. total.
- Slice and serve.

Some of the variations on this meatloaf is to include ½ cup of sautéed onions and /or a tablespoon of curry powder.

Joe Cannon's Favorite Meatloaf

This is my favorite! Takes about ½ hour to prepare and 1½ hours to cook.

Whenever my friend Joe comes to town, he always requests this meatloaf. In fact, he is the one who gave me the recipe, which I understand he obtained from the chef at Friday Harbor in the San Juan Islands of Washington State. If I did not include it in my cookbook, I might just lose a friend!

And this is the one I use when in a meatloaf cook-off. It is rather lengthy to make and has a lot of ingredients.

Yields enough for 10 people, but very good cold as leftovers.

INGREDIENTS:

1 3/4 lbs Black Angus ground beef

½ lb ground veal

¾ lb pork sausage

3 eggs, beaten

1½ cups bread crumbs

3/4 cup ketchup

3/4 cup heavy cream

½ cup brandy

1½ tbsp Worcestershire

3 oz butter

3 green onions, thinly sliced

1 yellow onion, ¼" chopped

3 stalks celery chopped

1 tbsp minced garlic

1 tbsp salt

1½ tsp ground black pepper

1 tsp white pepper

3 bay leaves

1 tsp cumin

1 tsp nutmeg

1 cup mushroom gravy

¼ cup chopped parsley

INSTRUCTIONS:

— Melt the butter in a large sauté pan over medium heat Add the onions, celery, bell peppers, green onions, garlic, Worcestershire sauce, brandy, bay leaves, and all the seasonings. Sauté until the vegetables are tender and the mixture starts sticking to the pan, about 20-30 minutes, stirring occasionally and scraping the pan bottom well. Stir in the cream and ketchup. Continue cooking for about 2 minutes. Remove from heat and allow mixture to cool to room temperature. Remove bay leaves.

- In a large mixing bowl, place the ground beef, veal and pork, add the beaten eggs, cooked vegetables, and the bread crumbs. Mix by hand until thoroughly combined. Place mix into 4" deep pan(s). Shape into loaf(s). Bake in a 350° oven for 35 minutes, then raise heat to 400° and continue cooking for 35 minutes longer. When done, top should be brown and firm to the touch. Internal temperature should be 135°.

- Let sit at room temperature for 10 minutes, then holding the top, drain the grease. Let sit for another 2 hours at room temperature in the pan to cool. After cooling, hold the top and drain any excess grease.

- Remove loaves from pans carefully.

LAMB

Lamb is my favorite of all meats. It is very tender and should usually be cooked medium rare. A lamb is a young sheep, less than one year old. One of the reasons I like lamb so much is that it is not as commercialized as beef or pork and therefore not feeder lot raised or injected with growth or other hormones.

I lived in New Zealand for a year and there the countryside is inundated with sheep. Lamb and mutton (older sheep) were mainstays of their diet. An interesting little factoid about New Zealand when I was there is that the population was about 2.5 million people and 25 million sheep. It seemed everyone had some sheep. I don't think people there had lawn mowers; they just kept a couple of sheep in the yard. It worked well - no grass cutting and no fertilizing.

Leg of Lamb

My specialty is to get a leg of lamb, deboned and butterflied—cut in half lengthwise—and put on the barbeque.

INGREDIENTS:

1 leg of lamb (about 5 lbs.)	1 tsp salt
Have the butcher debone and	1 tsp freshly ground pepper
butterfly for you.	1 tbsp oregano
1 garlic clove (not the full bulb!)	

DIRECTIONS:

- Heat the grill or oven to medium heat (350° oven)
- Cut most of the fat off the meat, and punch holes in it with a fork
- Mix the salt, pepper, and oregano together and rub into the meat
- Place on grill or in oven for 1¼ hours. Check internal temperature with an instant thermometer -when it reaches 130° the meat will be medium rare.
- Remove from heat and let it rest for about 15 minutes. Carve and plate.

Lamb Chops

Easy and delicious! Serves 4.

Here is a copy of the recipe I received from my friend Alan that I mentioned in the Introduction about how he wowed his then girlfriend -now wife.

Bob:

Dinner was fun. Look forward to our next one. Here is the "Seduction Dinner" recipe:

- Take a "French cut" rack of lamb and use a sharp knife to cut small cross-hatched slices into the fatty side of the rack.
- Rub into the cuts a paste made of the following ingredients and allow the rack to marinate for three hours (while you go to work or work on your date)

¼ cup garlic, finely minced

½ cup Durkee mustard sauce

6 shallots, finely chopped

1/8 cup fresh rosemary, finely chopped 1tbsp Balsamic vinegar

- Roast in the oven for 30 minutes at 350°, fatty side up.
- Serve with roasted fingerling potatoes, spinach in olive oil, and a nice French Margaux (Bordeaux).

Works almost every time! Regards, Alan.

TITILLATING LAMB SKEWERS

Serves 2 or 4: Fun, sex appeal, and easy!

Can be broiled in the oven or barbequed on the grill.

INGREDIENTS:

1 lb leg of lamb, boneless and cut into 1" cubes (2 lbs for 4 people)

½ tsp each of thyme, oregano, and rosemary: all finely chopped

1 tbsp olive oil

1 onion, medium-sized and cut into quarters

Salt and pepper to taste

2 or 4 metal or wooden skewers

DIRECTIONS:

- Preheat oven or grill to medium heat (about 350°) Mix all ingredients except the onion pieces together, including the lamb.

- Thread the pieces of lamb onto soaked wooden or metal skewers, alternating with the onions.
- If broiling, smear the bottom of a baking pan with the oil and place the meat on it and into the oven. Cook for about 6 minutes.
- If grilling, rub the grill with some oil and put the skewers on it, turning occasionally to make sure all sides are browned.

Osso Buco

Serves 4

Osso Buco literally means "hole in the bone." I make this recipe frequently during the winter as it is a great dish to serve on a cold, blustery night.

This is another one of Chef Lynn's recipes. Oh so good.

INGREDIENTS:
For the *meat:*

4 lamb or veal shank pieces cut
   1½ to 2" thick
   Tell your butcher it is for Osso
   Buco and have him tie them.

¼ **cup flour**
¼ **cup olive oil**

For the sauce:

1 large onion, chopped
1 tsp olive oil
1 tsp butter
1 carrot, chopped
1 stalk celery, chopped

2 garlic cloves, chopped
1 cup dry red wine
1-14oz can peeled and chopped
   tomatoes
Salt and pepper

DIRECTIONS:

The meat:

- Preheat oven to 350°
- Season the veal with salt and pepper to taste.
- Dip the meat into the flour to coat on all sides, shaking off the excess.
- Heat the oil in a large skillet over medium heat Sauté the meat on both sides to seal in the juices
- Transfer the meat to a casserole dish just big enough to contain it.

The sauce:

- In the skillet, sauté the onions in the oil and butter over medium heat until the onion is transparent.
- Add the carrot, celery, and garlic, sauté for 5 minutes Add the wine, and the tomatoes with their juice, stir until well mixed.
- Pour the sauce over the meat and place the casserole dish, covered, in the preheated oven for 1½ hours Uncover the casserole for the last 30 minutes.
- Plate and spoon the sauce over the meat.

GREMOLATA

This is a garnish usually put on top of Osso Buco.

It is simple to make and adds a further dimension of taste.

2 tsp lemon zest　　　　　　　**1 tsp finely chopped parsley**
1 garlic clove

- Mix the three ingredients together and sprinkle on top of the meat.

LAMB RAGOUT

Serves 4 and a little left over:

Probably my favorite Lamb dish. Recipe courtesy of my friend Sandra.

I have made this on a number of occasions and everyone raves about it.

INGREDIENTS:

2 lbs lean lamb cut into 1 1/2"
   cubes
¼ cup flour
½ tsp salt
¼ tsp pepper
¼ cup olive oil
1 ½ cups consommé

1/3 cup dry sherry
1 garlic clove, crushed
1 large orange
1 lb fresh sliced mushrooms
2 tbsp fresh lemon juice
1 tbsp chopped parsley

DIRECTIONS:

- Mix together flour, salt and pepper, coat lamb pieces. In a large frying pan, heat oil.
- Brown lamb on all sides to seal in the juices Stir in the consommé, sherry, and garlic
- Transfer the oven-safe frying pan (if you have one) into the oven, or put lamb mixture into a two-quart casserole. Cover and bake in a 350° oven until tender – about 1 ½ hrs.
- If cooked in covered frying pan, transfer to your oven-safe covered casserole that you can serve the dish in.
- (It is best to do the main oven cooking the day before you want to serve the lamb, to allow it to tenderize.) Let lamb cool, put in the cold garage or refrigerator overnight. Bring the mixture up close to room temperature, then reheat in oven an hour before serving, or do in advance then add to the lamb mix:
- Sauté the onions until translucent Sauté the sliced mushrooms

— Add to the lamb, and sprinkle with lemon juice and chopped parsley. Serve over fresh egg fettuccine!

Quick Pan Sauce

Easy

Once you have cooked the meat, remove from pan and use a little
white or red wine to scrape the bottom of the pan with a wooden
spoon and remove all the little brown bits left from the cooking. Let
the sauce thicken and then add a little butter. If desired, you can add a
little flour to help thicken the sauce.

I use the term "a little" in this recipe, as it depends on how much you
want to make. Obviously the more sauce you want, the more wine you
will add.

CHAPTER VIII
THE MAIN EVENT - CHICKEN

Chicken is one of the most versatile and easy-to-cook foods. There are literally hundreds of ways to cook chicken. In fact, one of the more difficult tasks in writing this book was to make choices and eliminate so many of my favorite chicken recipes. My advice to you is when stumped for a decision on what to cook, choose chicken. It is hard to screw up a chicken dinner.

The first decision to make is whether you are going to cook the bird whole or in pieces. If you wish to cook it whole, the best way to do so is by roasting. Once cooked, of course, you will need to know how to carve the bird. This is not difficult; you just need to understand the anatomy of chickens and where the joints are so you can easily cut it apart. In fact, I recommend cutting the bird in half before cooking as it reduces the cooking time to approximately one-half and there is no need to "truss" or tie up the wings and legs. To do this, cut between the legs and shoulder joints and then between the breasts so you end up with two approximately equal halves of the bird. However, if you are going to roast the chicken by the second roasting recipe, cutting it in half before cooking will not work.

A little hint here that will make cleanup a lot easier is to line the pan with a sheet of aluminum foil. This will prevent all the drippings from messing the pan and being cooked onto it.

Care must be taken when handling raw poultry. The flesh can contain certain bacteria such as salmonella. Whenever possible, keep the raw birds in the sink or other confined areas which will make it easier to wash and clean after you have prepared the chicken for cooking. Be sure to wash your hands as well as all surfaces that have come in contact with the raw meat with hot, soapy water.

Store poultry in the refrigerator. If you are not going to cook it within two days, freeze it. Frozen chicken will last for about six months. To thaw keep in refrigerator for about 12 hours, or for a quicker thaw, put in a sealable plastic bag and submerge in cold water.

ROASTING

This is a method of cooking in which you place the food item in an uncovered pan in the oven. It produces a well-cooked exterior and moist interior. Roasting requires relatively tender pieces of meat or poultry, as it tends to dry out the food. For less-tender food, a moist cooking method such as braising should be used.

THE NAKED CHICKEN

This is probably one of the easiest ways to cook chicken. The following recipe I got from a friend who is a chef in the Napa Valley of California. He claims it is the favorite way to cook chicken of Thomas Keller, one of the most famous American chefs. It is very simple and very delicious.

INGREDIENTS:

1 3-lb chicken   2 tsp paprika

3 tbsp butter   Salt and pepper

DIRECTIONS:

– Put oven rack in lower position and preheat to 400°.

- If you are going to cut the bird in half (as suggested above) do so now. Wash and dry the chicken. (Be sure to remove the gizzard package from inside the body cavity.) Rub with butter.
- Rub both the inside and outside of the chicken with a generous amount of salt and pepper.
- Sprinkle the paprika on the outside (skin side) of the bird.
- Make sure the chicken is at room temperature before you start to cook it.
- Place in oven and roast for 60 minutes, if cooking the bird whole.
- If split, cook for about 30 minutes. You can tell when the chicken is properly cooked by piercing the thick part of the leg. If the juice that runs out is clear, then the bird is done. If pink, cook for another 10 minutes and recheck.
- Remove from oven and let stand for 10 minutes to cool off. Carve and serve with potatoes and vegetables.
- Some variations on this recipe is to put four smashed garlic cloves, some lemon skins, and a twig of rosemary in the roasting pan when cooking the chicken.
- Another variation is to drape the chicken with bacon slices and let the fat and flavor of the bacon saturate the chicken during cooking.

ERECT CHICKEN AKA "BEER CAN CHICKEN"

This recipe is so easy it is embarrassing! It is called "erect" chicken, as it looks like it is standing up while roasting. It is one of my favorite ways to cook chicken and I do it often. Instead of roasting, you can also cook this on the grill.

INGREDIENTS:

½ can of beer (what you do with the other ½ is up to you).

1 whole roasting chicken (3-4 lbs)

1 tbsp dry poultry rub

1 tbsp each of salt and pepper

DIRECTIONS:

- Preheat oven or grill to 400°
- Remove the gizzard package from inside the bird Rinse well with cold water, pat dry - inside and out.
- Mix the salt, pepper, and dry rub together and rub generously the inside and outside of the chicken.
- Insert the ½ beer can in the butt opening of the chicken and stand the bird upright so that the can and the two legs are supporting the chicken.
- Place in the oven or grill for about one hour. You can tell when the chicken is fully cooked by piercing the thick part of the thigh with a sharp knife and if the juices run clear, it is done. If the juices are pink, return the bird to the heat for another 10 minutes and then test again.
- Once removed from the heat, let the chicken cool for about 10 minutes and then carve and serve.

ROASTED CHICKEN WITH HONEY AND SOUR PUSS

INGREDIENTS:

1 whole chicken (3 lbs)

1 cup honey

1 tbsp soy sauce

2 lemons, one squeezed for

juice, and one cut in quarters

2 sprigs rosemary

2 garlic cloves

Salt and pepper to taste

DIRECTIONS:

- Preheat oven to 400°
- Combine the honey, soy sauce, and lemon juice in a small bowl
- Wash and pat dry the chicken (remember the health advice about handling uncooked poultry).
- Place bird on an aluminum-lined baking dish and tuck the wings under Rub the cavity with salt and pepper.

- Place the rosemary, lemon quarters, and garlic inside the bird. Brush the honey glaze over the outside of the chicken.
- Place in the middle of the oven and roast for 60 minutes.
- Test for doneness by piercing the thick part of a thigh. If the juice is clear, the chicken is done. If the juice is still pink, return chicken to oven for another 10 minutes and then check again.
- When the bird is done, let rest for 10 minutes before carving.

CHICKEN - GRILLING (BARBEQUING)

The term "barbeque" is often used synonymously with grilling. It is the method of applying heat to food over a metal grate that is placed above a heat source such as charcoal, wood, rocks, or just a gas fire. It is very popular in outdoor cooking.

Chicken is one of the easier foods to cook on a grill. Caution here though, as the skin has a tendency to burn quickly on too hot a fire.

Easy Grilled Chicken with Barbeque Sauce

(Serves 4)

INGREDIENTS:
4 Chicken breasts (bone in)   1 cup Barbeque sauce
Salt and pepper to taste

DIRECTIONS:
- Heat the grill to about medium. This can be determined by the "Rule of Fours." That is, if you can hold your hand about four inches above the heat source for about only four seconds, the heat is probably right.
- Place the chicken pieces on the grill for about 5 minutes, then turn.
- Spread the barbeque sauce on the cooked part of the chicken and

let the other side grill. If you coat the side to be cooked, the sauce will have a tendency to burn.

— Grill for another 5 minutes and serve.

There are many variations to this recipe in that you can use a wide variety of sauces. For example, a chili sauce with vinegar and horseradish, or a combination of equal parts honey and Dijon mustard with chopped fresh dill for garnish. Also, there are many commercial marinades available in your grocery store for use on barbequed chicken. The choices are vast.

DELICIOUS BREASTS

(Serves 2 or 4)

No need for a discussion of the title!

INGREDIENTS:
(double everything if you are making this for 4 people)

2 Tender chicken breasts (boneless, of course) Don't they always come in pairs!	2 tbsp capers 1 fresh lemon 4 sprigs of fresh dill 1 tsp paprika

DIRECTIONS:
— Preheat oven to 400°.
— Be sure the wash and pat dry the breasts.
— Place on a baking sheet lined with aluminum foil (the aluminum foil is to make cleanup much easier).
— Squeeze the lemon juice on the breasts and sprinkle with paprika. Place i n oven for about 10 minutes, then flip the breasts and repeat

with the lemon juice and paprika.

- Return to oven for about another 10 minutes.
- Test for doneness by slicing one breast in half to see if cooked all the way through.
- Place the dill sprigs on top of the breasts along with the capers. Return to oven for 2 - 3 minutes
- Serve warm.

An alternative to roasting the chicken is to use the broiler part of your oven and place the chicken near the top of your oven. Be careful not the burn the chicken, as broiling cooks the outside very fast and leaves the inside less cooked.

THE FRENCH KISS: A DELIGHT ON YOUR TONGUE

CHICKEN PIECES IN MUSHROOM AND TARRAGON SAUCE

(Easy)

I was recently at a most fascinating dinner party in Paris where the hostess served this dish. To say it was delicious is an extreme understatement! I certainly had seconds and even could have had thirds but was too embarrassed to ask. She made the recipe for 14 people, but here is my simplified version pared down for two or four persons. She served it with asparagus and mashed potatoes.

INGREDIENTS:

4 pieces of boneless chicken: can be a mix of breasts and thighs, skin on or off.

½ can cream of mushroom soup

½ cup chicken broth (low sodium)

¼ cup fresh tarragon leaves

1 tbsp olive oil

DIRECTIONS:

- Preheat oven to 350°
- Brown the chicken pieces in a skillet, using the olive oil.
- Place browned pieces in an oven proof baking dish Pour in the soup, broth, and tarragon leaves.
- Bake in oven for 30 minutes and serve.

ENHANCED BREASTS (OLIVE-STUFFED)

Serves 4. Very easy.

This recipe I got from my friend and wonderful chef, Lynn. She says she knows it works—whatever that means.

INGREDIENTS:

4 boneless chicken breasts -with skin

1 cup brine-cured green olives, pitted and chopped

2 tbsp butter

¼ cup whole almonds with skin

2 tbsp chopped fresh flat leaf parsley

DIRECTIONS:

- Rinse chicken and pat dry
- Cut a 2" long horizontal slit in the thickest part of each breast.
- Stuff the slit with 1and ½ tsp of olives, then season with salt and pepper.
- Heat 1tbsp of butter in a large skillet over medium heat until melted.
- Add almonds to melted butter and cook for about 5 minutes. Transfer cooked almonds to a cutting board to cool.
- Increase heat to medium-high, add chicken breasts to skillet skin side down onto remaining butter in skillet and sprinkle with re-maining olives.
- Sauté breasts until skin is golden brown (about 10 minutes).

- Turn breasts over and cook over medium heat until cooked through (about 5 minutes more).
- Transfer to platter and keep warm. While chicken is cooking, chop almonds.
- Add remaining butter to skillet plus 3 tbsp of water, and heat, stirring until butter is melted.
- Stir in almonds, parsley and pepper to taste. Spoon sauce over chicken.
- Serve with green salad of butter lettuce with balsamic dressing.

PARMESAN-CRUSTED CHICKEN

Serves 4. Very easy.

INGREDIENTS:

4 boneless, skinless chicken breasts

½ cup mayonnaise

¼ cup grated parmesan cheese

4 tbsp Italian seasoned dry bread crumbs

DIRECTIONS:

- Preheat oven to 425°.
- Combine mayonnaise and cheese.
- Spread on chicken, then sprinkle with bread crumbs. Bake in lower part of oven for 20 minutes.

EASY CHICKEN CORDON BLEU

Serves 4.

Regular Cordon Bleu Chicken requires stuffing the chicken breasts, but here we will top the breasts with the ingredients.

INGREDIENTS:

4 boneless, skinless chicken breasts

1 cup heavy cream

½ cup white wine

1 cup shredded Gruyère cheese

2 tbsp Dijon mustard

4 slices baked deli ham

1 tbsp minced fresh tarragon

1 tbsp olive oil

1 cup panko bread crumbs

DIRECTIONS:

- Place oven rack at lowest level, and preheat oven to 450°. Rinse and pat dry the chicken pieces.
- Heat the olive oil in a large skillet over medium heat. Brown chicken on both sides, (about 3 minutes each side), then place chicken in ovenproof pan Put the wine, cream, half the mustard, tarragon, salt and pepper to taste in the skillet, and place on low heat.
- Spread the remaining mustard on each breast, with one piece of ham on top of each, and mound with a quarter cup of cheese.
- Sprinkle bread crumbs over each piece of chicken. Bake chicken for about 20 minutes
- Remove from oven, pour sauce onto the plates and place chicken on top of sauce. Serve warm.

CHICKEN CACCIATORE

If you were British, it sounds like you are trying to run for public office.

This is such a classic chicken entree and is fairly easy to make. I usually make it for my book club when it is my turn to host the group. However, the recipe that follows is scaled to feed 2 - 3 people.

INGREDIENTS:

6 pieces of chicken (can be a
   mixture of breasts and thighs)
   skin-on or skinless, but
   deboned
½ tsp each of salt and pepper
1 tbsp olive oil
1 medium-sized onion, chopped

2 garlic cloves, chopped
1green bell pepper, chopped
1 cup dry white wine
1 can diced tomatoes (14oz)
¼ cup low sodium chicken
   broth

DIRECTIONS:

- Rinse and pat dry the pieces of chicken.
- Heat the oil in a large skillet.
- Salt and pepper then brown both sides of the pieces of chicken (about 5 minutes per side). Remove from pan.
- Place the onion, garlic, and bell pepper in the skillet. Cook for about 10 minutes.
- Pour in the wine and scrape the brown bits from the bottom of the skillet. These little bits add a lot of flavor.
- Add the tomatoes and their juice to the skillet and cook until the liquid is reduced to about half (about 10 minutes).
- Add the chicken back in and cook for another 40 minutes.
- Remove chicken and further reduce the sauce by letting it boil until reaching the desired thickness.
- Plate the chicken and pour the sauce over the chicken.

Easy Coq Au Vin (Chicken In Wine)

Serves 4.

Probably my favorite chicken dish. Easy to make, very tasty and oh so tender.

INGREDIENTS:

6 chicken thighs, skin on and bone in 2 tbsp olive oil

6 garlic cloves, minced

1 medium onion, sliced

1 cup low sodium chicken broth

1 cup dry red wine (or white wine if you prefer)

¼ cup chopped flat leaf parsley

DIRECTIONS:

– Rinse and pat dry the chicken, sprinkle with salt and pepper. Heat oil in large skillet over medium heat.

– Brown the pieces of chicken, skin side down (about 5 minutes). Remove chicken from skillet, cook the garlic and onion 5 minutes.

– Add the wine and broth, cook until liquid is reduced in half Return chicken to skillet and cook with the sauce, loosely covered with aluminum foil, for 25 minutes. Plate and sprinkle with the chopped parsley.

Cornish Game Hen

(With emphasis on breasts and thighs)

For two people

This is one of my favorite main dishes to cook for two or four people. It is very easy and delicious. A Cornish Game hen is actually not a game bird. It is a domestic hybrid chicken which grows to 2-2.5 lbs. in about four weeks. I thought you would like to know that the breed develops rather large, firm breasts and has short, slender thighs. Both are very tasty if the proper amount and type of heat is applied. Also they are very tasty if stuffed in the proper fashion. They are readily available at any self-respecting meat department.

INGREDIENTS:

1 Cornish Game Hen

Olive oil

Salt and pepper

2 garlic cloves Paprika

4 sprigs thyme

DIRECTIONS:

- Preheat the oven to 350°F.
- Cut the bird in half by cutting on both sides of the backbone and one cut along the chest.
- Place in an oven proof skillet, skin side up. Sprinkle with salt and pepper, olive oil, and paprika (the paprika will help create a dark-brown crusty skin).
- Place two whole garlic (with skin on) cloves in the skillet Drape each piece of hen with a sprig of thyme.
- To plate, put a half of the bird on each plate along with some roasted fingerling potatoes and a vegetable of choice.
- And there, my friends, you have created an elegant and very tasty dinner.

CHAPTER IX

SEAFOOD - FISH

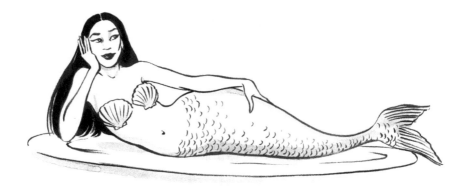

There are many varieties of fish that are very good and easy to cook.

I will mention a few of the more popular types here, as the cooking method is so similar for all of them - and all very easy. They include salmon, trout, tuna, cod, halibut, sole, bass, tilapia, sand dabs, and sablefish (Alaska black cod).

INGREDIENTS:

2-4 fillets of whatever kind of fish you select (one fillet per person)

1 tbsp olive oil

1 thin slice of butter

Salt and pepper

1 tsp capers (optional)

1 lemon, cut into wedges.

DIRECTIONS:

- Melt a little butter in a saucepan and add a tablespoon of olive oil. Lightly salt and pepper both sides of the fish.
- Place the fillets in the hot pan and sauté for about 2 minutes.
- Flip the fillets and cook for another 2-4 minutes, depending how thick they are and how well cooked you like your fish.
- Put the capers (if using them) in the saucepan for the last minute of cooking. Serve with the wedges of lemon.

One evening, a friend of mine was visiting from Vermont and we were going skiing for the next few days. My buddy decided to get some fish to cook up for the ladies we had invited for dinner. Well, that cheap son-of-a-gun went to the grocery store and bought a whole trout for each of us. He neglected to get any seasoning or lemons, etc. I told him I would get him for that, so I took a bottle of Chardonnay he had purchased and poured the whole thing into a deep frying pan and poached his four fish. He could not believe I would use a good bottle of wine for that. However, the fish really tasted great!

SALMON

Salmon is one of the most popular and healthy fish foods you can eat.

However, there is a strong caveat! Buy only Pacific salmon, as it is wild caught. Atlantic salmon is farm raised and is fed a lot of hormones and other food supplements for faster growing and color. Also, it is raised in a confined area in which all the droppings contaminate the water.

I do love wild caught salmon - and it is really easy to cook! Remember, this is written by a real fisherman.

Roasted, Pan Fried, or Grilled Salmon

Serves 2 or 4 or more. Very easy.

Ingredients:

2 or 4 Salmon steaks. About 6 oz each and about 1" thick I prefer the pieces cut from the fillet with the skin on as opposed to the steaks cut crosswise from the fish.

1 tbsp butter per piece of salmon
1 lemon per steak, half juiced, the other half cut into wedges
Salt and pepper to taste

DIRECTIONS:

- All these recipes could include a marinade for the salmon, of which there are many commercially available at your supermarket. I much prefer not to use any marinade as the salmon is so tender and tasty all by itself and many times the marinade overpowers the delicate taste of the fish.
- However, if you do prefer to marinate, it is very simple. Pour the marinade into at least a 3" deep dish along with the salmon. Put in refrigerator for at least one hour. Turn over half way through.
- If roasting, preheat oven to 350°.
- Melt the butter and add the lemon juice.
- Put salmon on an oven proof baking sheet, skin side down, and sprinkle with salt and pepper.
- Pour butter and lemon juice over steaks.
- Put in oven for about 6 to 7 minutes (the best way to tell if the fish is cooked sufficiently is when the white, fatty substance comes to the surface).
- If grilling: The procedure is the same, except preheat the grill to medium and wipe it down with an oil-soaked paper towel.
- No need to turn the steaks if fillets. If center cuts, then turn once.

– If pan frying: The procedure is still the same, except turn the burner to medium heat and let the pan warm up. Then pour a little of the butter in the pan and put in the fish. If pan frying the salmon, I find it best to put the steaks in skin side up first for about three minutes, then turn over for another three minutes. This way you will get a nice crispy top on the fish.

All these methods for cooking salmon should be served with a nice fresh salad or freshly cooked vegetables, and perhaps some baby roasted potatoes, couscous, or pasta with a white-wine butter sauce.

CHILI SALMON

Serves 2 or 4. Easy.

If you like salmon and you like chili -you'll love this!

INGREDIENTS:

2 or 4 salmon filets –6 oz each with skin on
½ cup chili powder
1 tbsp olive oil
1 lemon, cut into wedges

½ cup seafood seasoning (available in most supermarkets; if not, you can use Old Bay Seasoning, also available at most supermarkets).

DIRECTIONS:

– Combine the chili powder and the seasoning, then rub over the salmon.
– Place in an oven proof skillet and pan fry skin side down for about three minutes. Turn the salmon over and put in a preheated 400° oven on an oiled baking sheet for eight minutes. (Remember, to make it easier for you to clean, put a sheet of aluminum foil lightly

oiled on the baking sheet before you place the salmon on it).

— Serve with the lemon wedges.

Salmon Kebabs with Lime and Rosemary

Serves 2 or 4. Easy!

Given to me from Chef Michelle at Seven Mile Lodge on the west coast of Vancouver Island.

INGREDIENTS:

2 or 4 salmon fillets (about 6 oz each) skinned	2 tbsp olive oil
	Salt and pepper
2 garlic cloves	½ lime - juiced
3 - 5 sprigs fresh rosemary	½ lime thinly sliced

DIRECTIONS:

— Cut salmon into 1" cubes, place in a shallow container, and sprinkle with salt and pepper.

— Finely chop the garlic and the leaves from one sprig of rosemary. Place in a bowl or jar with the olive oil and lime juice, and whisk until blended.

— Pour the marinade over the fish and turn the cubes to make sure they are well coated. Then let it soak for about ten minutes.

— Preheat the grill to medium.

— Put the fish cubes on the skewers (my preference is to have extra rosemary sprigs and use these as your skewers, without the leaves) and grill for about five minutes, turning the fish to make sure all sides are grilled.

— Heat the remaining marinade in a small saucepan.

— To serve, arrange the skewers on a plate, pour the heated marinade over the fish, and serve with the lime slices and a sprig of rosemary.

POACHED TUNA IN OLIVE OIL

Serves 4. Easy.

This is one of my favorite ways to serve tuna. It is easy and makes for a very nice presentation. Also, it is very healthy. I learned this while vacationing in Southern France at the home of very special friends who own an art gallery. It is one of the widest art collections I have ever seen. In any case, his wife makes this dish whenever there are visitors coming to their private gallery.

INGREDIENTS:

4 Ahi tuna fillets, 6 oz each and 1" thick

4 cups regular olive oil (not virgin)

1 sprig rosemary

1 garlic clove

1 cup green salsa

DIRECTIONS:

- Season tuna with salt and pepper, both sides
- In a deep frying pan over medium heat, combine the oil, garlic, and rosemary. Carefully place the tuna fillets in the oil and cook for about 5 minutes, turning once if needed.
- Remove tuna and place on paper toweling to drain the excess oil.
- Cut tuna into :½ inch thick slices and serve with grilled baby potatoes, cherry tomatoes, and olives.

Seared Tuna Kebabs

Serves 2. Very easy. Ingredients:

½ lb fresh tuna, cut into six 1"
  cubes
½ cup of your favorite
  vinaigrette salad dressing
(for example, mustard,
  cucumber, or lemon
  vinaigrette)
2 cups mixed salad greens

½ cup cherry tomatoes
½ oz pitted kalamata olives
1hard-boiled egg (optional) cut
  into 6 wedges
2 skewers (if wood, soak in
  water for a few minutes so
  they will not burn when
  cooking)

DIRECTIONS:

- Pour ½ the vinaigrette into a resealable plastic bag. Add the tuna cubes and marinate for 15 minutes.
- Thread three pieces of the tuna onto each skewer (discard marinade).
- In a large skillet over high heat, sear the tuna on each side until light brown but still very rare in the middle (about one minute per side).
- Prepare the salad greens on a plate with the cherry tomatoes, olives and egg wedges - if using.
- Pour the remaining vinaigrette over the salad and place tuna on top.

Tuna from the Can

Serves 4. Very easy.

Ingredients:

1can (8 oz packed in oil) Tuna,
  drained and broken into
  chunks

½ of 8 oz jar roasted red peppers
1 onion, diced
1tomato, chopped

¼ cup Pine Nuts

¼ cup olive oil

Salt and pepper

DIRECTIONS:
- Toast the pine nuts in a large skillet for about 2 minutes (until they are slightly brown). Transfer to a plate.
- Put the olive oil and onions in the skillet and cook until they are translucent (slightly cooked -about 5 minutes).
- While the onions are cooking, coarsely chop the red peppers and add to the onions along with the tomato pieces
- Stir occasionally until the tomatoes are soft (about 3 minutes). Transfer the cooked vegetable mixture to a medium-sized bowl. Add the tuna and pine nuts to the veggies and mix.
- Season with salt and pepper as desired.
- Serve with thinly sliced toasted French bread.

SEARED SESAME TUNA

Serves 4. Easy.

INGREDIENTS:

4 Ahi tuna steaks, about 6 oz each and 1" thick

2 tbsp olive oil

1 cup mixed black and white sesame seeds

Salt and pepper

DIRECTIONS:
- Lightly salt and pepper the tuna steaks, then press in the mixture of sesame seeds evenly over the surface.
- In a heated skillet over high heat, pour in the oil and then place the tuna steaks in the pan.
- Sear for 1minute on each side.
- Remove from pan, thinly slice, and plate.

There are a number of sauces you can serve with this tuna—a soy sauce and wasabi mixture is delicious.

Another great combo is to serve with a salad with wasabi dressing.

Grilled Tuna with Salsa

Serves 2 or 4. Very easy.

INGREDIENTS:

2 or 4 Tuna steaks, 6 oz each
   and cut 1 inch thick

2 limes

½ cup tomato salsa 2 tbsp olive
   oil

Salt and pepper to taste

DIRECTIONS:

- Heat grill to medium.
- Lightly oil the grill with an oil-soaked paper towel.
- Brush the tuna steaks with the remaining oil and season with salt & pepper.
- Squeeze the juice of one of the limes over the tuna. Place the tuna on the grill for about one minute per side. Plate the steaks, spoon the salsa around the tuna.
- Serve with a lime wedge.

CHAPTER X
A LITTLE ON THE SIDE

POTATOES

A basic standard of the American diet!

BAKED & TWICE BAKED

Easy. 5 minutes prep, 1 hour cooking. 1 potato per serving.

The baked potato is probably the easiest and most common way to cook a potato. Simply get one medium-sized russet potato per person, wash and rub the skin, pierce the skin with a couple jabs of a fork, rub with an oil (olive, butter, or other kinds of cooking oil) and place in a 350° oven for about one hour (or 4 minutes per potato in the micro-wave). I usually wrap each potato in foil before putting in the oven. This helps to keep the skin a little softer and the potato meat more

99

moist. You can tell if the potato is cooked through by taking a sharp pointed knife and inserting into the potato. If the knife slides in easily and meets no resistance, then it is properly done cooking.

To serve, discard the foil - if used, make a slice about ½ way deep in the potato along the longitudinal axis, squeeze it from both ends to open the slit, garnish with butter, sour cream, diced chives, and crumbled cooked bacon (optional). Sometimes I add sautéed onions (see recipe below). Serve warm.

The twice-baked potato is certainly one of my favorites. Everything is the same in preparation and cooking, up to the point where you take it out of the oven and remove the foil. At this point, cut the entire potato in half lengthwise, and scoop out the flesh into a bowl. Save the skins as you will reuse them to "twice bake." Mix in 2 tablespoons sour cream, 1 teaspoon butter, chopped chives, and the bacon per potato. Mix all ingredients well and refill the half skins of the potatoes.

Put back in the oven and let bake again for about 20 minutes or until the top is crispy. Serve half of a potato per person.

MASHED POTATOES

Easy. Serves 4.

INGREDIENTS:

4 large Idaho potatoes　　　**4 tbsp butter**
½ cup whole milk　　　　　**Salt and pepper to taste**

DIRECTIONS:
— Peel and cut the potatoes into small pieces.
— Fill a large saucepan with water and a teaspoon of salt. Bring to a boil.

- Put peeled and cut potatoes into the boiling water for about 20 minutes.
- Remove the cooked potatoes from the water and place in a mixing bowl.
- Add the butter and milk, and mash with a fork or potato masher until you achieve the consistency desired.
- Add salt and pepper to taste.

These mashed potatoes are terrific with some Horseradish mixed in. I suggest you start with a tablespoonful first, mix well, taste, and then decide if you wish to add more horseradish - but one tablespoon at a time!!!

A further suggestion for your mashed potatoes is to mix in some grated cheese (cheddar or similar hard cheese). Again, the amount depends on taste.

POTATOES AU GRATIN

Easy. Serves 4.

I would be remiss if I did not include a recipe for Potatoes au Gratin for my friend Jim. This is by far his favorite side dish.

INGREDIENTS:

2 lbs potatoes	¼ cup Parmesan cheese, shredded
1 pint cream	
4 eggs, yolks only	1 tbsp minced shallot
½ cup Gruyère cheese, shredded	I clove garlic, minced

DIRECTIONS:
- Preheat oven to 350°. Grease a square baking dish.

- Mix the cream, eggs, shallot, and garlic. Peel and thinly slice the potatoes.
- Place ½ the slices of potato in the baking dish and cover with ½ the cream mixture.
- Combine the two cheeses and spread ½ on top of the potato/cream mixture.
- Spread the remaining potato slices evenly over the previous contents in the baking dish. Pour on the remaining cream mixture, then sprinkle the rest of the cheese on top.
- Cover with a sheet of foil and place in the preheated oven for 40 minutes.
- Remove the foil and continue baking for another 15 minutes or until brown on top.

ROASTED POTATOES WITH ROSEMARY

Any kind of potato can be roasted. I like to add some fresh rosemary sprigs to the roasting pan, as it instills a very pleasant flavor.

INGREDIENTS:

1 potato per person (medium sized)

2 tbsp cooking oil

2 sprigs fresh rosemary

Salt and pepper to taste

DIRECTIONS:

- Preheat oven to 400°.
- Wash and scrub the potatoes well. Cut potatoes into about 2" cubes.
- Grease a baking sheet or baking dish with 1 tbsp oil.
- Place the cut potatoes in a large bowl, pour the remaining oil over them, and toss gently to coat.
- Spread the potatoes on the baking sheet or dish and sprinkle with salt and pepper,

- Cut the rosemary sprigs into about 2" lengths and spread around the potatoes
- Place in oven for 30 minutes and then check for doneness by inserting a pointed knife. If it meets little or no resistance, then they are done. If not, put back in oven and keep checking every 10 min.

GRILLED POTATOES

INGREDIENTS:

1 potato per person

1 tbsp sour cream per potato

1 tsp butter per potato

1 pinch chopped chives per potato

DIRECTIONS:

- Heat grill to medium. Wash and scrub each potato.
- Place potato on grill for 30 min.
- Turn potato over and grill other side for another 30 min.
- Slit potato lengthwise and open up.
- Dress with butter and sour cream, and serve warm.

GREEN VEGGIES

BRUSSELS SPROUTS

Two ways.

Brussels Sprouts (B.S.) have a bad rap, in my mind. It is a delicious vegetable and can be cooked very easily. The reason many people do not like them is because of the strong taste. Just like liver and spinach, as kids we did not really like many strong- tasting foods.

Boiled

The easiest way to cook Brussels sprouts is to boil them -but don't overboil them!

INGREDIENTS:

1 lb Brussels sprouts, washed	2 tsp toasted pine nuts
2 quarts water	¼. cup grated parmesan cheese
1 tbsp salt	

DIRECTIONS:

- Boil the water in a large saucepan and add the salt.
- Trim the hard ends of the Brussels sprouts then cut an "X" in the base. This will help cook the vegetable faster,
- Place the "B.S." in the boiling water for about 5 minutes.
- Remove from water and let drain a minute or so.
- Plate, add salt to taste, sprinkle with the parmesan cheese and toasted pine nuts.

Roasted Brussels Sprouts

This is my preferred way to serve brussels sprouts. The roasting adds so much more flavor than boiling. However I do "parboil" the B.S's first. By parboiling I mean adding the veggie to boiling water for about three minutes. This will start the cooking process and soften them up for roasting.

Once parboiled let the B.S. cool, then slice lengthwise in half. Place cut side down on an oiled sheet of aluminum foil, sprinkle with olive oil, salt lightly, and roast in a 350° oven for about 30 minutes.

After cooking, place the B.S. in a large bowl, add crumbled bacon bits, roasted pine nuts, and grated parmesan cheese. Toss well and serve warm.

Cauliflower & Broccoli

Both of these are very versatile vegetables and generally interchangeable in most recipes. Cauliflower comes in a variety of colors, but white is by far the most common. Broccoli is a rich green color. Both can be cooked many different ways, some of which I will describe below.

Cauliflower comes wrapped in its own green leaves with a thick pale stalk, as does broccoli. Remove the leaves and stalk, and then cut the florets from the core.

I prefer to steam these vegetables first to soften them a bit, and then either roast or sauté. In addition, they can be boiled, pan fried, stir fried, or broiled. One trick I have used very successfully is to steam the cauliflower, then put in a blender and blend well. The finished product will look exactly like mashed potatoes, taste like cauliflower, and have a lot less carbs! I was surprised how well the blended cauliflower was appreciated. And it is easier to make than mashed potatoes.

One head of broccoli or one head of cauliflower will serve between three or four people - depending on how generous a portion you serve.

I like to serve broccoli either with sautéed onions (recipe below) or by itself with a mayonnaise sauce.

Cauliflower can be served with roasted red peppers (available in your grocery store in a jar), or mixed with grated cheddar cheese.

The basic steaming technique for cauliflower and/or broccoli is to put a couple of inches of water in a pot and either with a double boiler or steamer in the bottom, bring to a boil. Place the head of cauliflower or broccoli in the pot and cover. Let steam for about 15 -20 minutes. You can tell when the C/B is done as it is tender when pierced with a sharp pointed knife.

Oven-Roasted Cauliflower Florets

Easy. Serves 4.

Roasting caramelizes the cauliflower and brings out a very special sweet taste.

INGREDIENTS:

1 Head cauliflower	**1 lemon, cut in quarters**
2½ tbsp olive oil	**Salt and pepper to taste.**

DIRECTIONS:
- Cut the florets off the stalk of the cauliflower. Preheat oven to 400°.
- Spread the florets onto a baking sheet. Sprinkle with the olive oil.
- Roast in the oven for about 30 minutes. Serve with the lemon wedges.

ONIONS AND MUSHROOMS

A classic all-time favorite of mine. I do these for almost all main courses except maybe seafood. But for meat and poultry, it is a standard and everyone loves the mixture.

SAUTÉED ONIONS AND MUSHROOMS

Very easy. Serves two.

INGREDIENTS:

1 medium-sized yellow onion
½ lb white button mushrooms

1 tbsp cooking oil
Salt and pepper to taste

DIRECTIONS:

- Peel and dice the onion.
- Clean the mushrooms, cut off the base of the stems, and cut the caps into quarters.
- Heat a saucepan with the oil over medium fire.
- When pan and oil are hot, place the onions in first and let sauté for about 5 minutes, then add the cut mushrooms to the onions.
- Cook for another 5 minutes, and then you are ready to serve over your meat or poultry.

CARROTS, PEAS, AND PEARL ONIONS

This is very easy and a colorful dish to serve with almost any main course. Pearl onions are those little white or red round onions usually sold in a mesh bag at almost all grocery stores.

INGREDIENTS:

1 small bag pearl onions
3 medium- sized carrots

1 bag frozen green peas.

- Parboil the pearl onions, let cool and then peel off the skin.
- Peel and slice the carrots into 1" thick pieces,
- Boil a large pot of water and add all the ingredients,
- Let cook for about 5 minutes. Do not overcook, as the veggies will become mushy.
- Drain and serve.

EGGPLANT AND ZUCCHINI PARMESAN

Easy. Serves 2 -4

A very simple but delicious vegetable dish that can easily be a main course.

INGREDIENTS:

2 Japanese eggplants
2 zucchinis
1 can (14oz) pasta sauce

2 cups shredded parmesan cheese
½ cup torn basil leaves

DIRECTIONS:

- Preheat the oven to 400°.
- Cut the ends off both the eggplants and the zucchinis and then slice into thin strips lengthwise.
- Pour half the sauce into a baking dish, spread a layer of the eggplant and zucchini on top, and sprinkle with ½ the cheese and basil.
- Repeat the same process over again.
- Put in the oven to bake for about 30 minutes.

RATATOUILLE

The King of mixed vegetable dishes!

This is really a casserole and is easy once you break the process down into certain stages. All it takes is a little patience and love.

The main ingredients are onion, eggplant, zucchini, tomatoes, bell peppers, and a variety of herbs. Also included are whatever other vegetables one has left over and can include even potatoes and mushrooms.

The recipe that follows is one of the easier ones which will take about 1 ½ hours, including one hour of cooking.

INGREDIENTS:
(Chop all the veggies into bite-sized pieces).

1 medium-sized onion

1 medium-sized Japanese eggplant (other eggplants need to be salted and sweated)

2 small zucchini

1 each of red, yellow, and green bell peppers cored and seeded,

2 large red tomatoes

3 cloves crushed or minced garlic

2 tbsp olive oil

1 tsp each of thyme, rosemary, and basil Salt and pepper to taste.

DIRECTIONS:

- In a large skillet or roasting pot, pour in ½ the oil. Mix in all the vegetables, herbs, salt and pepper.
- Cook over a medium flame for 30 minutes, stirring occasionally.
- Pour in the remaining oil, if needed, after about
- ½ hour and cook for another 15-30 min.

PASTA

Everybody knows spaghetti. It is a member of the "pasta" family. It seems that every area in Italy has its own pasta specialty. I know about 20 different styles of pasta and they all vary primarily in the thickness and shape.

Store-bought dried pasta comes in many varieties. It is quite good and easy to cook. Just add it to boiling water - but not too long, as it will get starchy and sticky. It is better to undercook it just a little, as it will continue to cook in its own heat even after you have drained the water from the pot. This is called "al dente" i.e. almost fully cooked!

PASTA WITH TOMATO SAUCE AND PARMESAN CHEESE

Very easy. Serves as few or as many as you wish.

INGREDIENTS:

Pasta: Style and quantity dependent on the number you wish to feed.

Large pot of boiling water

1 tbsp salt

½ cup tomato sauce per person

¼ cup grated parmesan cheese per person

DIRECTIONS:

- Add the salt to the pot of boiling water.
- Put in the pasta and let boil for about 5 minutes.
- Drain the pasta from the pot.
- Pour into a large bowl along with the tomato sauce and cheese.
- Mix well and serve while still warm.

This is the same way to cook any style of pasta, and with many varieties of sauce.

Orzo With Artichokes & Pine Nuts:

Easy, serves 4 as a side dish or 2 as the main course.

Orzo is a pasta that is shaped like long grain rice. It seems softer than other types of pasta and is very good with many different sauces or vegetables. Here I am suggesting the use of canned (or bottled) artichoke hearts, as they are already peeled and seasoned -which makes preparing this dish quite easy.

INGREDIENTS:

2 cups orzo. (Available in most grocery stores in the pasta section.)

2 cups artichoke hearts –either whole or pieces

¼ cup pine nuts

3 tbsp olive oil

3 tbsp vinegar

Salt and pepper to taste

DIRECTIONS:

- Place orzo in a pot of salted boiling water until cooked to al dente. Drain into a large bowl,
- Gently roast the pine nuts in a frying pan until golden brown. Be careful not to burn, as they cook very quickly.
- Mix all ingredients together and toss well.

MAC & CHEESE

An American standard! I think many of you were probably weaned on Mac & Cheese. I know I was!

INGREDIENTS:

4 cups salted water

1 lb pasta shells: many types are available

½ stick butter

2 cups milk

2 cups grated cheddar cheese

2 tbsp flour

Salt and pepper to taste

½ cup each of bread crumbs and parmesan cheese.

DIRECTIONS:

- Preheat oven to 400°.
- Boil the water in a large pot.
- Cook pasta in the boiling water to al dente. Drain pasta and let cool.

- Heat the milk, but do not let it boil.
- Add the butter until it is melted. Stir in the flour and mix well.
- Add the cheese and continue stirring.
- Pour the mixture over the pasta and mix further. Pour all into a greased baking dish.
- Sprinkle the bread crumbs and parmesan cheese on top.
- Bake for about 20 minutes.

CHAPTER XI
A HAPPY ENDING - DESSERT

(Dessert)

"Life Is Uncertain, Eat Dessert First!"

I heard this saying many years ago and have not forgotten it. I think it makes a lot of sense. Sometimes I don't feel like a whole meal but am a little hungry and desire something sweet. Well, DESSERT is just the answer.

Dessert can run the entire spectrum of very simple to very elaborate. In this chapter I will start with the very easy and simple recipes and end up with a more fancy one.

Ice Cream (or Sorbet) and Fresh Fruit

Very easy.

Serves as many as you wish - from two to twenty!

INCREDIENTS:
- 1 cup or appropriate shaped glass per person
- 2 small scoops ice cream (or sorbet) per person
- 1 spoonful blueberries
- 1 spoonful red berries (raspberry, strawberry, or blackberry)
- 2 small cookies

DIRECTIONS:

- Place the ice cream in the bowl or glass. Top with your selection of berries.
- Add the cookies to the plate and serve with a spoon.

There! Is that easy, or what!

CARAMEL FLOATS

Easy. Serves 4.

1 cup sugar

2 teaspoons lemon juice

3/4 cup heavy cream

2 tbsp bourbon

2 tbsp butter

2 scoops vanilla ice cream per person

2 cans root beer

DIRECTIONS:

- In a saucepan, bring the sugar and lemon juice to a boil over medium heat, stirring to dissolve the sugar.
- Continue cooking until mixture is a caramel color.
- Remove from heat and stir in the heavy cream and the bourbon. Return to heat and whisk until smooth.
- Melt in the butter.
- Put two scoops of the ice cream in each glass and fill with root beer.
- Drizzle with the caramel sauce.

Super Simple. Healthy Hot Cocoa

Very easy. Serves two.

INGREDIENTS:

3 teaspoon unsweetened cocoa
  powder

3 teaspoons sugar

Pinch of salt

2 cups skim or low fat milk

DIRECTIONS:

- Combine all ingredients in a saucepan and heat GENTLY (do not let it boil).
- Stir frequently until the cocoa is just beginning to steam. Pour into mugs and enjoy.

Affogato

Very easy. Serves 2 4

Just a fancy name for a very simple dessert.

INGREDIENTS:

2 scoops ice cream per person

1oz espresso or strong coffee
  per person.

DIRECTIONS:

- Put the ice cream in a small dessert bowl and pour the hot coffee over it.
- Serve!

Now was that too difficult?

A lot of variations can be done with this highly involved recipe.

For example, I often will pour a liqueur over the ice cream instead.

My favorite is Frangelico or Cointreau.

CHRIS' POPPY SEED CAKE

Easy, serves 6.

My hat is off to Chris, an old Rugby buddy turned chef.

INGREDIENTS:

1 pkg yellow cake mix

1 pkg instant coconut cream
  pudding mix

½ cup vegetable oil

¼ cup poppy seeds soaked in
  1 cup warm water for about 15
  min.

DIRECTIONS:

- Mix all together,
- Put in a greased and lightly floured pan (Chris uses a bundt pan).
  Bake @ 350° for 30 -40 minutes.

Key Lime Pie

Easy, serves up to eight.

Key Lime pie is one of my absolute favorite desserts. Whenever I see it on a menu, it is an automatic order.

The recipe here is very simple, but to really be a traditionalist, you should make it with a graham cracker crust. I am giving you both the store-bought crust version (very easy) and the more elaborate " graham cracker" crust.

<u>Simple version:</u>

INGREDIENTS:

1 store-bought pie crust (in refrigerator compartment)	1cup fresh Key lime juice
2-14oz cans evaporated milk	4 egg yolks
Grated zest of 2 Key limes	½ pint whipped cream (optional)

DIRECTIONS:
- Mix together all the filling ingredients except the whipped cream.
- Pour into the pie crust.
- Bake in 350° oven for about 15-20 minutes. Let cool and center will gently set as it cools.
- Chill pie and then serve.

Graham Cracker Crust

6 large graham crackers	½ stick unsalted butter
1 cup sugar	½ cup slivered almonds

DIRECTIONS:
- Preheat oven to 350°. Butter a 9" pie pan.

- Pulse all ingredients in a food processor.
- Press crumb mixture into the pie pan and cover the Bottom and sides.
- Bake about 10 minutes, and let cool. Pour in the pie filling and refrigerate.

BLUEBERRY LADY BAIT

Very easy. Serves 8-10.

I made this one time for my book club, as we were having an outdoor meeting and invited our ladies to attend. All the guys had to bring a plate of food. My duty was to bring the dessert. This was so popular that on the next occasion which the ladies attended it was actually requested by a number of the gals, along with the recipe. They were really surprised when it was revealed how simple it was to make.

INGREDIENTS:

1 box prepared angel cake mix
½ cup sugar
½ teaspoon ground cinnamon

½ cup frozen or fresh blueberries (if frozen, do not thaw)

DIRECTIONS:

- Prepare the cake mix according to instructions on box. Fold in the frozen or fresh blueberries.
- Pour into greased and floured baking dish; spread evenly. Mix the sugar and cinnamon together.
- Sprinkle a few blueberries on top, as well as the mixture of sugar and cinnamon.
- Bake in oven according to package directions.

CHAPTER XII

B & B
(BED & BREAKFAST)

"Oh yes, of course I'll still respect you in the morning!"

To paraphrase the great comedic English writer A.P. Herbert in his classic work <u>Uncommon Law</u>:

"A critical period in a relationship is breakfast time."

The best response I have ever heard regarding breakfast was when this fellow asked his lady friend as he was getting up to get her some coffee, "How do you like your eggs?" She said, "Fertilized!"

Breakfast can be one of the most romantic meals of a date.

You can gain a lot of points depending on how you handle the situation.

After a great evening of good company, conversation and food, what could be better for the finale!

And to paraphrase what I said earlier— it is a shorter distance to the bedroom from the kitchen table than from a restaurant.

So what do we do the morning after!

The first and most common activity is to get up and make the fair lady a cup of coffee, a cup of tea, or a glass of fruit juice and bring it back to her in bed. A huge winner is always the Champagne Mimosa recipe that is included in Chapter III (i.e. orange juice and Champagne). She will be grateful forever.

Making coffee is very simple. What you should have is a coffee machine. There is a broad spectrum of coffee makers (not to mention instant coffee—which is terrible, in my opinion). There are many levels that you can jump into regarding the making of a good cup of coffee. Purchase whole roasted coffee beans and grind them fresh, or buy already ground beans and put them in a coffee machine with water and boil away. It is really quite easy. Be sure to have some sugar/artificial sweetener and milk or cream on hand. One option worth looking into is this new type of coffee machine in which you buy "pods" of coffee and insert them into the machine, which already has water. By turning the machine on, it automatically starts heating the water; you then place the coffee pod accordingly, press the button, and out comes some very good coffee in the cup you have placed appropriately on the machine. There are at least two well-known makers of these machines, and each company also sells the pods. They are Nespresso and Keurig. Both of these brands are readily available in all kitchen supply stores and department stores.

If her preference is tea, you can simply boil some water, pour it into a cup and put in a tea bag. Let it soak for a few minutes, then discard the tea bag, and you have your cup of tea.

This too might need some sweetener and milk or cream.

I am going to assume that all of you know how to make toast, open a container o yogurt, make a smoothie and fix a bowl of cereal with fruit. But if you want to show a level of flair, consider stepping it up with eggs, pancakes and breakfast meats.

So let's move to the next level of making breakfast. This can involve some cooking or none. That is your choice.

COOKED BREAKFAST

(From the simple to the more involved.)

EGGS: The cooking of eggs is really quite easy. But don't be in too much of a hurry when doing so. This will be explained in the respective recipes for each kind of cooked eggs.

Eggs cooked almost any way are usually served with a sprinkling of salt and pepper and some toast.

SOFT BOILED

INGREDIENTS:

1 or 2 eggs per person   **Bread for toasting**

Salt and pepper   **Pot for boiling water**

DIRECTIONS:

Bring a pot of water to a boil and then back the heat down so that you have just the occasional bubble coming up in the water (a slow boil). If you use too much heat the water will boil rapidly and cause the eggs to bump into each other thus possibly cracking the shells and having the egg whites seep out into the cooking water. Put the eggs in the slow-boiling water for three minutes. This will produce perfectly cooked soft boiled eggs.

As a caveat, let me say that if you are going to boil a large number of eggs and you take them right out of the refrigerator, you may want to let them cook for about another minute longer.

PRESENTING:

There are a number of ways to serve the soft boiled eggs. My preference is to cut about one-quarter off the top of the shell and then eat the contents with a spoon. There are special "soft boiled" egg dispensers available on the market but I don't think you have to go to that extent. Or you can scoop out the contents of the shell into a small cup or onto a plate and eat with toast.

The eggs are usually served with buttered toast.

POACHED

INGREDIENTS:

1 or 2 eggs per person

Toasted bread or English
  muffins

Salt and pepper

Pot or pan for boiling water

DIRECTIONS:

– Poaching eggs is similar to boiling them, except that the eggs are out of their shells.

– Bring a pot or pan of water to a boil and the reduce the heat slightly so as to produce a very slow boil. Add a tablespoon of white vinegar to the water before heating it. This will help keep the egg intact while cooking. Some cooks even turn the heat off as soon as they put the eggs in the water and let the eggs cook in the heated water. This takes about twice the time than if you left the heat on a slow boil. A perfectly poached egg will still have the yolk a little runny. Don't overcook them! I personally much prefer poached eggs to any other type of egg. In order to keep the egg intact, I break the shell and put the uncooked egg(s) into a cup, which I then lower into the slowly boiling water.

There are wonderful egg poachers available for sale in most stores selling cookware.

I must confess I use one myself. These are pans in which you put water and bring to a boil then you put the unshelled egg into the small insert and place into the boiling water. Let the eggs cook to your desired doneness then just slide out of the little insert. They are very easy and convenient to use.

On a ski vacation a few winters ago, we were staying at a friend's house and they knew that my standard Sunday morning breakfast was poached eggs with bacon on toasted crumpets. (Crumpets are round baked English muffin like bread products that are magnificent with poached eggs, as they have small holes in the top which allow the broken yolks to soak in. They are available in some grocery store and bakeries). In any case, we did not have a poacher so I tried to make the poached eggs in just the boiling water. This was before I learned that you need to turn the heat down and bring the water to a slow boil before you put the eggs in. Well, the poached eggs turned out to be a disaster! I have since bought the hostess an egg poacher!

PRESENTING:

To serve, just turn the little cups in the egg poacher over on either the toast or plate, and if sprayed properly with cooking oil before putting in the eggs they will slide out easily.

FRIED

INGREDIENTS:

1 or 2 eggs per person
Bread for toast
Salt and pepper
Butter, olive oil or breakfast
  meat fat – such as bacon fat

Bacon, ham, or sausages (The cooking of these is described in this chapter under "Breakfast meats.")

DIRECTIONS:

- The finest fried eggs I've ever had were in Ohio when visiting friends. The lady of the house was kind enough to share her secret with me, and now I am going to share it with you.
- If you are serving with bacon or other breakfast meats such as ham or sausage, cook these in the pan first as they will provide some fat to coat the bottom of the pan and add some flavor to the fried eggs. If you are not cooking with any of the meats, place a little butter

or olive oil in the pan.

— Heat the pan on medium heat for about one minute. When the pan is hot, crack the egg(s) into the pan and let the whites cook through. If you are doing "sunny side up" fried eggs, cook until the yolk is the consistency you desire. If doing "over easy" fried eggs, flip the eggs over with a spatula and let the yoke cook a little. Remember, do not overcook the eggs, as they will become tough and rubbery.

Now for my friend's secret. She cooked bacon before the eggs and got a good amount of fat from it. She then fried the eggs in the bacon fat, but as they cooking she gently spooned the hot fat over the eggs. This provided beautifully cooked egg yolks and whites.

As to some variations, you could put seasoning such as basil, or oregano in the fat before the eggs. Some people recommend garlic, but this being the morning after, I do not recommend it.

Another variation, which is a nice touch, is to cut a circle in a piece of bread with a glass or cookie cutter. Then place the bread that has the cut-out circle in the frying pan, crack the egg into the cut-out circle and fry. Flip it over with a spatula if wanting "over easy" style fried eggs.

PRESENTING:
Slide the cooked eggs onto a plate along with the toast and bacon, ham, or sausages. Add a sprig of parsley.

SCRAMBLED

INGREDIENTS:

2 to 3 eggs per person Salt and
  pepper
1tbsp of either butter or olive oil

2 tbsp milk (optional)
Small frying pan

DIRECTIONS:

- Break the eggs into a small bowl and beat vigorously with a fork. If
you like your eggs a little runny, add the milk to the beaten eggs.
Sprinkle with salt pepper to taste. Add the oil or butter to the small
frying pan and heat until the oil thins out. Pour the beaten egg/
milk mixture into the pan and keep stirring with a spatula. This
will allow the runny part of the uncooked eggs to flow to the bottom of the pan and get cooked.

PRESENTING:

Once the eggs are done to yours (and her) liking, remove from the pan
and put on a plate.

Serve with toast and bacon or ham, or if so desired.

There are many variations regarding scrambled eggs. I like to make
them with smoked salmon. Sometimes I sauté up some onions and
mix them in with the eggs just before I cook them. Other variations
include chorizo and scrambled eggs, green onions (scallions) and eggs,
bell peppers (green, red, and/or yellow) chopped up and mixed in with
the eggs, asparagus with the eggs. Just let your imagination run wild
and I am sure you can come up with other very tasty combinations.

OMELET

There are so many ways to make a good omelet. The real key is to cook the eggs properly. Do not over or undercook them. The proper method is described below in how to prepare the omelet.

INGREDIENTS:
Same as for scrambled eggs plus whatever ingredients you want to add for the omelet.

This can include any kind of vegetables, meats, and cheeses.

Some suggestions as to what you can add to make it an omelet are:

- Shredded cheese and chives (many kinds of cheeses are suitable; for example: Gruyere, cheddar, fontina, goat cheese, etc.
- Sautéed onion and smoked salmon, (lox).

- Bacon and cheddar cheese

- Avocado and cherry tomatoes

- Prosciutto and fontina cheese

- Spinach and feta cheese

- Leeks and brie

- Sautéed vegetables (vegetarian omelette)

- Egg white and goat cheese

And the list goes on. It is only limited by your own imagination.

DIRECTIONS:

The cooking is the same as for scrambled eggs, except rather than stirring once they are cooking, you simply use the spatula to push back a side of the cooking eggs to let the uncooked part run into the bared portion of the pan. This will allow the runny uncooked part to cook. At this point you add whatever ingredients you choose for the omelet to ½ of the cooked eggs and let it/them warm up in the pan.

Once the egg(s) is cooked and the ingredients warm, fold the ½ that does not contain the filling over the part that does and slide onto a plate for serving.

FRITTATAS

A frittata is just an omelet with all the ingredients mixed up before you put it in the frying pan. I have made frittatas with almost any vegetables that were left in the refigerator, along with some cheese and even breakfast meats.

Here are some of the combinations I've used: Asparagus and goat cheese

Artichoke and leeks Italian sausage and onion

Potato, scallions, prosciutto, and Gruyere cheese.

The trick with frittatas is to not bum the underside but still get the top cooked. There are a couple of ways to do this that I have used. The first is to put the partially cooked mixture in the oven to broil. Or the second way, which is a little more tricky, is to flip the partially cooked frittata over on a flat dish and then slide it back into the frying pan. This allows what was the top uncooked portion to now be the new bottom in the pan and thus get cooked. When done, just slide it onto a plate, cut to desired size, and serve.

FRENCH TOAST

INGREDIENTS:

1 - 2 slices of thick cut bread per
person
1 - 2 eggs, beaten as for
scrambled above

Jam - strawberry, raspberry, etc.
Salt and pepper
1 tbsp butter or olive oil
Medium frying pan

DIRECTIONS:

– Cooking French toast is really quite simple. Heat the oil or butter in a frying pan. Beat the eggs as described above. Dip the bread into the beaten eggs and place in the heated pan.

– Once one side of the bread is cooked to your liking, turn it over and cook the other side.

PRESENTING:

You are now ready to serve with some jam

One time I tried to get fancy with my French Toast, so I took some sugar and put it a blender to make it like powdered sugar. I then sprinkled - very lightly - the powdered sugar over the toast. It was a nice presentation but did not add much to the taste of things.

An interesting variation on this is to make a "Banana Stuffed" French toast.

All you need to do is make two slices of French toast per person and then slice a couple of bananas lengthwise, and heat in a mixture of butter and sugar. Once the bananas are softened, slide between two pieces of the French toast, pour a little real maple syrup over it - and enjoy! A further variation of this is to coat the French toast with peanut butter and then put on the lightly cooked bananas.

Many other coatings can be used on the French toast. you are limited only by your imagination. For example, pear and cranberry compote, blueberry sauce, or spicy applesauce.

PANCAKES & WAFFLES

From the Box! This ia super breakfast food.

INGREDIENTS:

1 small box pancake mix.	**1 egg**
Available in any grocery store.	**1 cup milk**
This also will do for waffles.	**Butter**

Some pancake mixes require more or less of these and perhaps other ingredients. Read the ingredients required on the box before you buy it to make sure you have the right ones and enough of them.

Maple syrup. Get the real stuff as it is so much better than the corn syrup commonly pushed off as maple syrup. Having lived in Vermont for many years and made real maple syrup with my friends each spring, I promise you there is a HUGE difference. And it is well worth the small price difference!

Frying pan for pancakes, or Waffle iron

DIRECTIONS:
Follow the instructions on the pancake mix box regarding the quantities of ingredients required. Heat the pan over medium with some butter. Mix the ingredients in a bowl. Pour in a small amount of the mixed batter and let it spread out over the inside of the heated pan.

Additionally you can tell when one side is cooked and ready to flip over as the top of the batter will form little air bubbles and break open. When the batter around the little holes made by the bubbles appears dry, then flip. The same will not happen on the top side as it did for you what was then the bottom. No little tiny when cooking air bubbles to form or drying out of the batter. In order to cook this now bottom side correctly, you will have to occasionally take a peek at the underside. When it is a medium brown, your pancake is ready.

Cooking waffles is a lot easier, but you do need a waffle iron. These are readily available in most cooking supplies stores and are relatively inexpensive. Spray the waffle iron plates with a good cooking oil. You can use the same batter, but just pour it into the heated waffle iron, close the lid, wait until the batter stops steaming. Waffle is then ready.

PRESENTING:
Place on a dinner-sized plate.

I like to serve either my pancakes or waffles with butter, maple syrup and usually bacon, ham, or sausage. (The cooking of these is described in this chapter under "Breakfast Meats"). Serve these items on a small side dish and let your guest help herself to the quantity she likes.

A fun thing to do with pancakes is to try any one of a variety of toppings. You can put a jam or fruit on them, fried eggs, or just plain butter. They all taste good.

PANCAKES FROM SCRATCH

There are many pancake and waffle recipes. I am going to give you a simple but wonderful one which you can use as a base and then you can go on and experiment further when you feel confident enough.

QUICK AND EASY DORO'S STRAWBERRY PANCAKES:

This is a recipe given to me by my friend Doro, who insisted on making breakfast one morning. It was so good and easy that I convinced her to let me include it in this book. This is for two to three pancakes.

INGREDIENTS:
Frying pan or skillet 1 cup flour   1 tbsp sugar
2 cups milk (a little more if you   1 tbsp butter
   want the pancakes thinner   4 strawberries.
2 eggs

DIRECTIONS:
– Combine the eggs, sugar, milk, and flour and whisk until combined and still liquid.
– Melt butter in frying pan. Pour batter into pan to barely cover the bottom.
– Slice strawberries thinly and put into frying pan before the batter becomes too firm.
– Brown enough on bottom to bake berries into the batter.
– Flip over and brown the bottom. Fold over and add syrup.

- A nice addition to this would be a little strawberry syrup, or jam and butter.

BREAKFAST MEATS

Now we get back to some real cooking!

Breakfast meats include primarily bacon, ham, and sausage. Sometimes steak or chicken is also included.

BACON

In order to cook bacon, you need a frying pan and some sliced bacon.

All you do is put about four slices per person in the hot pan and cook until your desired degree of doneness is reached. Then remove the cooked bacon from the pan and place on a folded paper towel to drain the excess oil and fat from the bacon. you are now ready to serve on a plate with eggs and/or toast.

Bacon can also be cooked in a microwave or regular oven. This is a little tricky as the time for cooking varies considerably. Know what you are doing before trying either of these "oven" methods.

HAM

The cooking of ham is the same as cooking bacon. You need to buy some sliced ham and everything else is the same.

SAUSAGE

You can buy either patty-style sausage or link- style sausage. The patty ones are just (usually pork, beef and/or veal) in a hamburger patty shape. Link sausages are the more common type; hot dog-shaped and usually linked together by the casing.

It is the same to cook either style. Heat your frying pan and place the sausage into it. Cook to your desired degree of doneness. Serve as you would the bacon.

BREAKFAST STEAKS AND CHICKEN

Here I refer you to Chapter VII "The Main Event," which includes the cooking of meat.

EVEN FANCIER

This next recipe is one of my favorites. It was given to me by my friend Travis Fugate. He was born in Eastern Kentucky but now lives in Monterey, California where he is attending university, studying computer science. Travis is a wounded warrior from the Iraqi war. He was blinded by an IED while driving his Hummer.

His own description of how he got into cooking is very interesting.

"While recovering from my loss of vision due to injuries sustained in Iraq, I found joy and comfort in cooking. I never realized how dangerous a kitchen could be until I stepped into one without vision! With every small venture into the kitchen I came out feeling like I had accomplished something and boy, did I need this.

"After more than five years of blindness I now cook regularly in my own kitchen.

My favorite dishes are those that can be made using only one piece of cookware—a baking dish, large pot, or big skillet. I love cooking something nice and only having one dish to clean up afterwards.

"Bob, I can't wait to see how your book turns out."

CRANBERRY BAKE

(An upscale variation of French Toast)

Serves 4 - 6

You can prepare this easy breakfast or brunch dish the previous night and then most of your work is done before you need it in the morning.

INGREDIENTS:

Medium-sized baking dish 4 slices bread

1 tbsp melted butter

¼ cup dried cranberries

¼ cup chopped walnuts

4 eggs

½ cup milk

¼ tsp ground nutmeg

A few drops of vanilla extract

Sprinkling of salt

DIRECTIONS:
- Rub the bottom of the baking dish with a very thin layer of butter.
- Lay two slices of bread on the bottom and brush them with a thin layer of butter.
- Spread the cranberries and walnuts over the bread, and then cover with the remaining two slices of bread.
- In a small bowl, whisk together the eggs, milk, sugar, nutmeg, vanilla extract, and salt.
- Pour the egg mixture over the bread, making sure to soak the top layer completely.
- Cover and chill for at least two hours, or preferably overnight.

- When ready to bake, let dish come to room temperature. Preheat oven to 350°F
- Uncover and bake until golden brown and cooked through, about 45 min.
- Set aside for 5 -10 minutes, then serve.

I like this dish with a little real maple syrup on top.

ADDITIONAL FANCY SUGGESTIONS

Eggs Benedict

This is poached eggs served on a slice of Canadian bacon and toasted English muffin with hollandaise sauce.

Serves 2 people.

INGREDIENTS:

Egg poacher or pot for boiling the water Frying pan for cooking the bacon

Small sauce pan for warming the hollandaise sauce

(You can either make the sauce from scratch or buy it pre-made or dry mix.)

4 eggs

2 English muffins

2 slices of Canadian bacon or ham

4 tbsp hollandaise sauce (available in most grocery stores)

Salt and Pepper

1 tbsp butter

DIRECTIONS:

- Poach the eggs - as per instructions above, Toast the muffins and then butter them. Fry the bacon or ham.
- Plate the recipe by placing one slice of the cooked bacon or ham on each half of the buttered muffins, then putting a poached eggs

on top of each slice of cooked bacon. Spoon the hollandaise sauce over the eggs and serve.

— Serve with a cup of hot chocolate!

Now that you are able to make a nice breakfast for your guest, your day can start all over again!

The next step is up to you.

CHAPTER XIII
FINALE

That brings me to the end of my cooking suggestions for all my friends who wish to expand their repertoire for entertaining the ladies. I hope you have enjoyed the information I presented, and I hope you find it useful.

One last thing! I have done a lot of research for this book and have come across many, many interesting recipes. However there is one that stands out above all others. I would like to share it with you.

It is called "Jellied Moose Nose" and was printed in a cook book published by a branch of the Canadian government called *Northern Cooking* edited by Eleanor A. Ellis. I know this will sound like an Andy Borowitz newsletter, but it is not. The book is for people living "way up North."

If all else fails, and you really want to impress your lady friend, here is the secret! This is the most outrageous recipe I have ever come across.

I leave this you with and your good judgment.

Jellied Moose Nose

Upper jawbone of a moose	1 tsp salt
Onion; sliced	½ tsp pepper
Garlic clove	¼ c vinegar
1 tbsp mixed pickling spice	

- Cut the upper jaw bone of the moose just below the eyes.
- Place in a large kettle of scalding water and boil for 45 minutes.
- Remove and chill in cold water.
- Pull out all the hairs—these will have been loosened by the boiling and should come out easily (like plucking a duck).
- Wash thoroughly until no hairs remain.
- Place the nose in a kettle and cover with fresh water.
- Add onion, garlic, spices, and vinegar.
- Bring to a boil, then reduce heat and simmer until the meat is tender. Let cool overnight in the liquid.
- When cool, take the meat out of the broth, and remove and discard the bones and the cartilage. You will have two kinds of meat, white meat from the bulb of the nose, and thin strips of dark meat from along the bones and jowls.
- Slice the meat thinly and alternate layers of white and dark meat in a loaf pan.
- Reheat the broth to boiling, then pour the broth over the meat in the loaf pan.
- Let cool until jelly has set. Slice and serve cold.

I must confess I have not yet tried this recipe, mainly for lack of a moose nose... but, sometime, maybe.

The reference for the above mentioned book is:

Northern Cookbook from the Ministry of Indian Affairs, Ottawa, Canada, edited by Eleanor A. Ellis

It has been a very fun journey, over about three years, writing this cookbook for you guys. As my wife has said on numerous occasions, "I am tired of hearing that you are writing a cookbook. What I want to hear is that you have written a cookbook".

I should add that it has also taken its toll. I am now "thinner on top and thicker in the middle." Ah, but all in the name of fun and research.

Now let me return to my earlier caveats (as in the Introduction).

REMEMBER:

BE BOLD

BE CREATIVE

EXPERIMENT, DON'T BE AFRAID TO TRY DIFFERENT THINGS

GO NUTS

HAVE FUN

WEAR NICE UNDERWEAR

GET LUCKY!

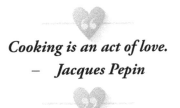

Cooking is an act of love.
— Jacques Pepin

—

One more word of wisdom from my lovely wife: "If all else fails, return to Chapter III."

APPENDIX
APHRODISIACS: THE FOOD THAT EXCITES

Ever since we humans have been preparing food, and maybe even before that, we have been trying to enhance our desires through what we eat. Food and desire are central to our thinking.

The term "Aphrodisiac" is used to describe any food that supposedly increases or arouses our sexual desire. It is named after the goddess of love and beauty in Greek mythology – Aphrodite.

There is a lot of controversy about whether such foods actually work. However, even if the science is not there to prove the chemistry of such claims, the fact that we think they work, is often sufficient for them to be effective. It has been said that our biggest sexual organ is the one between our ears. What is desire other than the hope we can fulfill our fantasies. And that's all in the mind.

With all that as a disclaimer, let me list some of the more common foods considered either by science or myth to be aphrodisiacs. Some of these are considered aphrodisiacs because of the chemical composition and the hormones they boost in our bodies. Others are considered aphrodisiacs due to their visual appearance.

- Chocolate: Probably the most well know which when consumed creates a sense of wellbeing. It is thought the chemicals in chocolate help promote the production of the feel good hormone – serotonin. However, there is some controversy about the actual chemistry at work.

- Oysters: One of the more joked about pseudo- aphrodisiacs. They are high in zinc which is supposed to help in the production of sexual hormones. Who knows?

- Asparagus: These contain high amounts of vitamin E and potassium which helps increase blood flow and increase the sex hormones. I think asparagus fall more into the category of "visual" aphrodisiacs than chemical ones.

- Avocados: More of a male aphrodisiac as they contain high folic acid which is a vitamin B and supposedly increases testosterone. I have heard that avocados are also symbolic of female reproductive organs and thus considered "visual" as well.

- Chilies: Considered to be an aphrodisiac as it stimulates the nerve endings on the tongue thus releasing adrenaline. Very spicy which warms you up and gets your heart pumping, i.e. increase blood flow.

- Strawberries and Cherries: Contain vitamin C which increases the sex drive and libido by helping in the production of chemical transmitters in the brain.

- Watermelon: Indirectly increase the nitric acid in the body which increase blood flow. Also, it is less filling dessert so you feel more active after dinner.

- Salmon: A fish high in Omega-3 fatty acids which helps in producing the sex hormones and develops libido.

- Almonds and Walnuts: Little did I know before my research on aphrodisiacs that I often vacation just a short drive away from the almond capital of the world – Fresno, CA. Many Mediterranean cultures have almonds in their pastries or serve them before a meal. They contain fatty acids that help in hormone production.

- Honey: One of the best all around foods, I think. Contains nitric oxide as well as Boron. Both of these help open blood vessels and blood flow.

- Pomegranate: The "Love Apple". Full of antioxidants which help blood flow to all parts of the body.

- Figs: Have high amino acid content which helps increase libido and stamina.

- Bananas: Contain enzymes that are believed to be aphrodisiacs as well as potassium which gives strength to muscles. But here obviously is a case of the visual being considered the stimulant.

- Coffee: We all know it as a stimulant which increases stamina and elevates the mood.

This list of aphrodisiacs is not meant to be all inclusive as many other foods also claim some amorous arousing qualities. However I tried to include the more common ones.